Dav

By United Library

https://campsite.bio/unitedlibrary

Table of Contents

Table of Contents 2

Disclaimer 4

Introduction 5

David Bowie 7

Biography 10

Space Oddity and early successes (1967-1969) 28

Metamorphosis: from "folk" to "glam rock" (1970-1971) 38

The Age of Ziggy Stardust (1972-1973) 50

Funk, "plastic soul" and *Diamond Dogs* (1974-1975) 55

The "White Duke" years and the Berlin trilogy (1976-1979) .. 59

Commercial and mass success (1980-1989) 66

The short period with the Tin Machine (1989-1990) 70

New experiments and the return to the past (1990-1999) 73

Musical style 87

Collaborations 90

Personal life 93

Discography 96

Videography 99

Other books by United Library 101

Disclaimer

This biography book is a work of nonfiction based on the public life of a famous person. The author has used publicly available information to create this work. While the author has thoroughly researched the subject and attempted to depict it accurately, it is not meant to be an exhaustive study of the subject. The views expressed in this book are those of the author alone and do not necessarily reflect those of any organization associated with the subject. This book should not be taken as an endorsement, legal advice, or any other form of professional advice. This book was written for entertainment purposes only.

Introduction

Immerse yourself in the extraordinary life and incomparable legacy of David Bowie, the iconic British singer, composer, and actor, in this compelling biography. Born as David Robert Jones on January 8, 1947, Bowie transcended the boundaries of music and art, leaving an indelible mark on the 20th century as one of its most influential musicians.

From his early struggles with local bands and a solo album to the groundbreaking success of "Space Oddity" (1969), Bowie's career has been a continuous journey of reinvention. The glam rock era saw the emergence of his eccentric alter ego Ziggy Stardust, who captivated audiences with hits such as "Starman" and "The Rise and Fall of Ziggy Stardust and the Spiders from Mars." His evolution continued with the "plastic soul" sound of "Fame" and "Young Americans," and later with the electronically influenced albums known as the Berlin Trilogy.

Bowie's impact extended beyond music; he became a cinematic force with roles in such films as "The Man Who Fell to Earth" (1976) and "Labyrinth" (1986). Reaching commercial peak with "Let's Dance" (1983), he navigated the 1980s and 1990s with various musical experiments and continued in his acting endeavors.

Revered for his chameleon-like ability to reinvent his musical persona, Bowie's journey culminated in his last work, "Blackstar," released just days before his death from liver cancer in 2016. This biography unravels the enigma of Bowie's artistic genius, exploring the highs and lows, musical transformations and cinematic contributions that shaped the legacy of the "rock chameleon

David Bowie

David Bowie, pseudonym of David Robert Jones (London, January 8, 1947 - New York, January 10, 2016), was a British singer-songwriter, multi-instrumentalist and actor.

A passion for music led Bowie to learn to play the saxophone when he was still very young. After participating in the formation of various bands, he achieved solo success in the early 1970s, spanning five decades of rock music and earning a reputation for perfecting the glam rock genre. Significant and fruitful were his collaborations with Tony Visconti and Brian Eno, veterans of early 1970s glam rock, with whom he established a strong and deep friendship that lasted many years.

Although not his main activities, Bowie also devoted himself to painting and film, working as an actor with directors such as Martin Scorsese, David Lynch, and Christopher Nolan. Among the various films in which he starred are *The Man Who Fell to Earth*, *Furyo*, *Miriam Wakes at Midnight*, *Absolute Beginners*, *Labyrinth*, *Basquiat*, *The Prestige*, and *My West*.

With approximately 140 million albums sold in his lifetime, David Bowie ranks among the top-selling artists and in 2007 was listed by *Forbes* magazine as the fourth richest singer in the world. Considered one of the most influential musicians in contemporary music, in 2008 he was ranked 23rd on the list of the hundred best singers according to *Rolling Stone,* which singled out *Life on Mars?*, *Space Oddity*, *Fame* and *"Heroes"* among his best songs. In addition, five of his albums are included in the list of the 500 best albums according to *Rolling Stone*. In 2019 Bowie was named "the greatest entertainer of the 20th century" through a poll conducted by BBC Two.

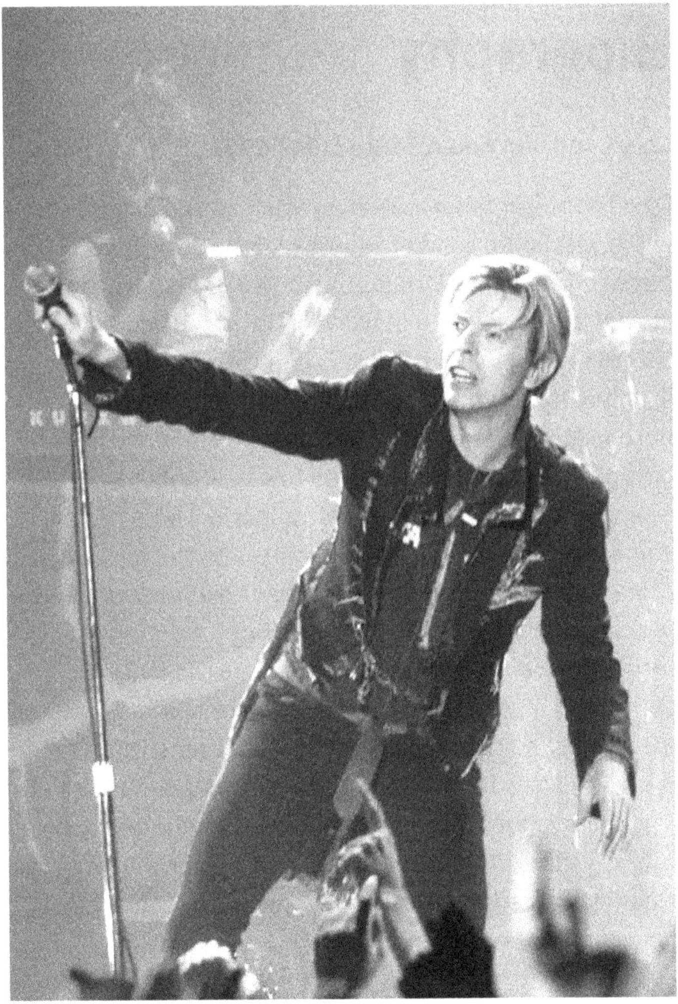

Biography

Childhood and Adolescence (1947-1961)

David Robert Jones was born in Brixton, a neighborhood in the vast south London suburbs, on January 8, 1947. His mother, Margaret Mary Burns, known as "Peggy," was a cashier at a local cinema, while his father, Haywood Stenton Jones, was a former soldier recently returned from the front who later became warden of Bromley Prison. At the age of six he moved with his family from his birthplace at 42 Stansfield Road to a new home in Bromley, a nearby south London suburb, where he immediately began to show an interest in the music that came from the United States. "*When I was very little I saw my cousin dancing to Elvis's Hound Dog,*" he later recounted, "*and I had never seen her get up and wiggle like that to any other song. The power of that music struck me so much.*" David began from school age to listen to records by Fats Domino and Little Richard and to cultivate a growing interest in rhythm and blues, skiffle and rock 'n' roll, as well as other art forms. When a teacher asked him what he wanted to be when he grew up, he replied that he wanted to be Britain's Elvis.

A key role in his musical education was played by his half-brother Terry Burns, born in 1937 from a previous relationship with his mother. "*Terry was the beginning of everything for me,*" David recounted years later, "*he read a lot of beat writers and listened to jazz musicians like John Coltrane and Eric Dolphy...while I was still in school, he was going downtown every Saturday night to hear jazz at different clubs...he was growing his hair out and, in his own way, he was a rebel... all this had a great influence on me.*" Suffering from paranoid schizophrenia and confined to the psychiatric ward at Cane Hill Hospital in Croydon from the 1970s until 1985, when he took his own life by throwing himself under a train, Terry would inspire the singer in several circumstances as evidenced by the 1970 album *The Man Who Sold the World* or songs such as 1971's *The Bewlay Brothers* and 1993's *Jump They Say.*

In 1958 David began singing as a chorister at St. Mary's Church with friends George Underwood and Geoffrey MacCormack, and the following year he received his first saxophone as a gift from his mother. Advised by Terry he began taking lessons from jazz saxophonist Ronnie Ross: "*For me, the saxophone represented the Beat Generation of the West Coast, that period of U.S. culture fascinated me very much. That instrument became an emblem for me, a symbol of freedom.*" Over the course of his career he would learn to play many instruments, showing more flair on rhythm guitar than solo.

Another formative experience in David's musical education was his brief employment in the Bromley record store, during which he became fascinated with the music of James Brown, Ray Charles, and Jackie Wilson, at that time still little known in Europe. In 1960 he joined a group of students at Bromley Technical High School interested in art, and his creative talents were encouraged by progressive teacher Owen Frampton, father of guitarist Peter Frampton, with whom he would later collaborate. Two years later the opportunity arose to join George Underwood in one of the school's musical groups, and David's artistic adventure began.

The pre-Deram years (1962-1966)

In mid-1962 David and Underwood joined with some students who had formed a group called The Kon-rads, which had been founded by Bromley Technical High School students Neville Wills and Dave Crook in early 1962; Underwood offered to sing for them and, in June brought David along to sing Joe Brown's *A Picture of You* and help out with vocals for a cover of *Hey! Baby* by Bruce Channel. David began to use his tenor sax and the Kon-rads had a revival. The first documented concert was held on June 16 at a school party. "The Kon-rads did covers of all the songs that made the charts," David recounted 30 years later. "We were one of the best cover bands in the area and we worked a lot."

At the end of the year Underwood left the group and was replaced by a new singer, Roger Ferris, while David Crook was replaced on drums by Dave Hadfield. The group's ranks were augmented by the arrival of Rocky Shahan on bass, guitarist Alan Dodds, and backing singers Christine and Stella Patton. "At *first I came in as saxophonist,"* David said, "*but then our singer Roger Ferris was beaten up by some greasers at the Orpington Civic, and that's when I took over singing.*" The Kon-rads played in youth clubs, parish halls and even had a brown corduroy uniform. David began experimenting with his attitude on stage and introducing new ideas to make the band more "appealing," changed the name to Dave Jay, inspired by the beat group Peter Jay and the Jaywalkers, and also began composing songs of his own, some of which were added to the group's repertoire that included songs such as *In the Mood*, *China Doll* and *Sweet Little Sixteen*. It was during this period that Underwood, during an altercation at school over a girl named Carol Goldsmith, punched him in the left eye and the ring he wore on his finger caused chronic traumatic mydriasis. The result was permanent dilation of the pupil, which would forever characterize his gaze and leave him with altered depth and light perception.

In August 1963 Decca Records manager Eric Easton invited the Kon-rads for an audition after seeing them in concert in Orpington. On August 30, at Decca's West

Hampstead studios, the group decided to perform *I Never Dreamed*, a song David had written based on news of a plane crash. In addition to writing the song's lyrics, 16-year-old David appeared as backing vocals and played saxophone on what is considered his first known studio recording. In any case, the audition was unsuccessful and contributed to his exit from the Kon-rads. Within a short time the Kon-rads became too limiting for David: "*I wanted to switch to rhythm and blues,*" he later recounted, "*but they didn't agree. They wanted to limit themselves to the Top 20. So I left.*"

After leaving Bromley Technical High School, David began working as an apprentice illustrator for the American advertising agency J. Walter Thompson. "I was a junior visualizer," he would recount in 1993, "it was an important qualification but I was really just making collages. And I never got a chance to prove myself because the agency was teeming with talent." A positive side of that job was meeting Ian, a fellow John Lee Hooker fan: "In a Soho store I found John Lee Hooker's album and one by Bob Dylan. I bought two copies of both and, since Ian had introduced me to John, I gave him the Dylan album. I discovered these two artists in one day. It was something magical... " The influence of the U.S. bluesman's music is evidenced by the name of the trio David would form after the Kon-rads with George Underwood on guitar and harmonica and drummer Viv

Andrews, The Hooker Brothers (although on some occasions they went by other names such as The Bow Street Runners and Dave's Reds & Blues). The band performed covers and earned a few gigs at Peter Melkin's Bromel Club and Ravensbourne College of Art, but it was short-lived and after a few gigs Andrews left. David and Underwood thus laid the groundwork for the trio with whom they would record their first record, the King Bees, a 45 rpm entitled *Liza Jane*. The group's name had been inspired by a song by bluesman Slim Harpo, *I'm a King Bee*. The other members, besides David and Underwood, were Roger Bluck, Dave "Frank" Howard and Bob Allen, guitar, bass and drums, respectively. "I can'*t even remember what their names were,*" he would confess in 1993, "*they were from North London and they were almost professionals. Pretty scary.*" However, he and Underwood, as the latter confided, soon assumed control of the band: "*We imposed our tastes on the others.*"

In the spring of 1964 David came into contact with manager Leslie Conn, who procured the King Bees an audition with Decca and a chance to record the single, as well as an evening at the Marquee Club and appearances on the BBC television programs *Juke Box Jury* and *The Beat Room.* Conn initially got the King Bees a gig at Bloom's wedding anniversary party in Soho. "It was all rather awkward," David recounted years later. They had time to play *Got My Mojo Working* and *Hoochie Coochie*

Man before Bloom yelled, "*Get them off! They're ruining my party!*" Auditioning with Decca turned out to be more satisfying, and a short time later allowed them to finally record *Liza Jane*. Thus, Bowie's first official 45 was released on June 5, 1964, albeit credited to Davie Jones with the King Bees, and the singer quit his job at the advertising agency. To promote the single, Conn procured the group a series of appearances at various London venues. David had the opportunity to make his first appearance at the Marquee Club, and on the BBC programs *Juke Box Jury* (June 6) and *The Beat Room* (June 27). However, the poor success of *Liza Jane*, which sold very few of the 3,500 copies printed, decreed the end of his militancy in the group.

In August he joined the Manish Boys, already active for four years and considered to be at the forefront of the so-called *Medway beat*, and at the end of the year he granted his first television interview: accompanied by flowing blond hair, in an effort to gain publicity he claimed to have founded an association called the "*International League for the Preservation of Animal Hair.*" Already active for four years, Johnny Flux, Paul Rodriguez, Woolf Byrne, Johnny Watson, Mick White, and Bob Solly were not exactly thrilled with David's arrival, as Solly himself said in 2000 to the British monthly *Record Collector*: "At first we didn't want to, but Conn replied, 'He's got a record deal, he just put out a record, and it might be an advantage for you.'" David assumed a position of dominance and turned the group toward rhythm and blues. On August 18, the *Chatham Standard* announced, " [...] another piece of news from the boys is that they are now accompanying Decca star Davie Jones, whose group, the King Bees, has dropped him." The following day David played for the first time with the Manish Boys at Eel-Pie Island, a famous jazz venue in Twickenham.

On October 6, the group made its first recording at Regent Sound Studios, where covers of Barbara Lewis' *Hello Stranger*, Gene Chandler's *Duke of Earl* and Mickey & Sylvia's *Love is Strange* were recorded. Although the possibility of making a 45 rpm was considered for the first track, none of the tracks were released. A month later Bowie gave his first major television interview although it had little to do with his music. By now accompanied by flowing blond hair, in an effort to gain publicity the singer claimed to have founded an association called the "International League for the Preservation of Animal Hair," and it was in his capacity as "president" that he found himself interviewed by novelist Leslie Thomas in the Nov. 2 edition of the British *Evening News* and *Star* newspapers (the title of the article was "Who's Behind the Fringe?"). On December 1, the group began a six-date tour in which they played as a backing band for Gene Pitney, the Kinks, Marianne Faithfull and Gerry and the

Pacemakers. With the exception of *Liza Jane* and *Last Night* (written by the Manish Boys and used as concert openers) the sound of their performances was mainly based on American blues and soul ranging between James Brown, Ray Charles and the Yardbirds.

The Manish Boys' recording career took a turn in early 1965 when the group was noticed by U.S. producer Shel Talmy, known for arranging and producing The Kinks' *You Really Got Me* and, a little later, The Who's debut album. As a result, on March 5 the band released the 45 rpm *I Pity the Fool* on Parlophone, to which the then-unknown session player Jimmy Page also contributed. The recording and mixing of the single did not meet with the approval of the other members, however, and the end result disgruntled much of the group. When on March 8 Leslie Conn managed to get them a TV slot on the BBC for the program *Gadzooks! It's All Happening*, David found himself involved in the second advertising campaign imprinted on the length of his hair. The *Daily Mirror* published an article titled "War over David's hair," and the following day the *Daily Mail* reported that the band had been kicked off the program and that David had stated, "I wouldn't get a haircut if the prime minister asked me to, let alone for the BBC." On the day of the broadcast, the *Evening News* published a photo of the most publicized pop singer of the week in the act of getting a haircut to appear on the program.

I Pity the Fool did not receive benefit from either the television appearance or the publicity that came with it, and David parted ways with the group after an argument over the appearance of his name on the single (the song had been attributed simply to the Manish Boys despite the fact that they had originally agreed to have it appear as the work of Davie Jones and the Manish Boys). Despite the failure of *I Pity the Fool*, producer Shel Talmy managed to get a contract with Parlophone. By April David was leading Lower Third. The band, which hailed from Margate and had formed in 1963, needed new members after three of its members left, and David auditioned at La Discotheque in Soho along with Steve Marriott, who soon left to form the Small Faces. In those days Bowie also auditioned (mostly at the Marquee Club) for other groups including the High Numbers, which would shortly explode as the Who. On May 17, 1965, a performance at the Grand Hotel in Littlestone officially gave birth to Davy Jones and the Lower Third, which included Denis "Tea-Cup" Taylor on guitar, Graham "Death" Rivens on bass, and Les Mighall on drums (later replaced by Phil Lancaster). "I think I wanted it to be a rhythm and blues group," Bowie said in 1983. "We used to do a lot of John Lee Hooker tunes and try to adapt his stuff to the big beat, without much success. But it was all the rage back then: everybody was picking a blues musician ... ours was Hooker."

The group released the single *You've Got a Habit of Leaving* on August 20, recorded at IBC Studios during a session in which two other demos (listenable in the 1991 *Early On* collection) were put on tape in addition to the B-side *Baby Loves That Way: I'll Follow You* and *Glad I've Got Nobody*. On the same day of the single's release, Lower Third opened the Who's concert at the Bournemouth Pavilion and David met for the first time Pete Townshend, another great source of inspiration for the English singer. Shortly thereafter he left Leslie Conn for his first full-time manager, Ralph Horton. This 45 also proved unsuccessful, and David dumped Leslie Conn for his first full-time manager Ralph Horton, whose first decision was to oversee the transformation of the four long-haired teenagers: decked out in the latest fashion pants and Carnaby Street flower ties, he forced them into a mod-style haircut and encouraged the use of hairspray. The latter novelty upset some members of the group but not David, who was already infatuated with the dandy image of the mods and their new spokesmen, the Who. Horton secured Lower Third a series of summer concerts, and the band began to behave like Roger Daltrey and Pete Townshend's group by smashing instruments at the end of performances. "We were known as the second most rowdy band in London," Denis Taylor recounted years later. On August 31 the Lower Third recorded demos of two songs, *Baby That's a Promise* and *Silly Boy Blue*, in which the influence of groups such as Kinks and Small Faces but also that of Motown r&b continued to be noted.

At this time the singer officially adopted the stage name "David Bowie" to avoid being confused with Davy Jones of the Monkees. He later recounted that he chose that name inspired by the hunting knives of the same name: "I wanted something that expressed a desire to cut short the lies and all that." Apparently, the inspiration came to David after seeing the 1960 film *The Battle of the Alamo*, in which knife maker Jim Bowie was played by Richard Widmark.

Ralph Horton did not prove to be the Lower Third's best buy in skill and financial ability so much so that it was he himself, aware of his own limitations, who contacted Kenneth Pitt, Manfred Mann's manager (and Bob Dylan's when he was touring Britain) and asked him to assist the Lower Third. Pitt declined, but advised David to change his name to avoid being confused with the Davy Jones who was becoming famous with the Monkees. A few days later, on September 17, 1965, David announced to the rest of the band that he would henceforth be called David Bowie. Shortly thereafter Bowie and the Lower Third secured a contract with Pye Records that would soon yield their first record with producer Tony Hath.

On Nov. 2, the band failed an audition for a BBC television program in which they played a rock version of *Chim Chim Cheree* (song from the movie *Mary Poppins*), *Out of Sight* (James Brown cover) and *Baby That's a Promise.* "A cockney type, not particularly original, a singer with no personality who sings the wrong notes and out of tune," was one of the committee's lapidary comments about Bowie.

1965 closed with the recording of three songs at Pye Studios in Marble Arch: *Now You've Met The London Boys* (reworked and released a year later as *The London Boys*), and what would be the A and B sides of the new 45: *Can't Help Thinking About Me* and *And I Say To Myself.* On New Year's Eve the group played with Arthur Brown in Paris and stayed for a couple of days. The release of the single was imminent, but David's preferential treatment during the publicity campaign was instrumental in creating a rift between him and the rest of the group. The knots came to a head on January 29, 1966, at the Bromel Club in Bromley, when the Lower Third refused to play after learning from Horton that they would not be paid that night. The band's disbandment left Bowie with a single to promote and no band to accompany him. Despite some encouraging reviews, the record (the first also released in the United States) was as much of a flop as those that had preceded it but generated enough interest to earn the singer his first interview on *Melody Maker* on February 26 and an appearance on ITV's *Ready Steady Go!* program, where he performed the song accompanied by a new band, The Buzz, on March 4.

David Bowie and the Buzz, namely John Hutchinson (guitar), Derek Fearnley (bass), John Eager (drums), and Derek Boyes (keyboards), had given the first of a series of live performances at Leicester University on February 10, 1966. About his meeting with Bowie, Hutchinson said years later, "I first met him after I had spent a year playing rhythm and blues with the Apaches in Gothenburg in 1965. I showed up for a very professional audition at the Marquee Club in Wardour Street, London, on a Saturday morning and it went well. I think David chose me because I was wearing Swedish clothes, a suede jacket, jeans and blue clogs-no one in England had seen stuff like that until then-and I think Bowie was impressed. I was also the best of the guitarists who showed up for the audition anyway!"

Three days after the TV appearance on *Ready, Steady, Go!* the band recorded *Do Anything You Say*, which would be released as a 45 on April 1 and credited to David alone, thus avoiding the misunderstandings present in previous groups. "From day one," said drummer John Eager, "we realized that we were actually David and his backing band." Ralph Horton contacted Kenneth Pitt again, and in the meantime the band began a series of concerts at the

Marquee Club, called the "Bowie Showboat," which would be held on Sunday afternoons until June 12. After attending the second of these concerts Pitt officially became Bowie's manager and Horton assumed the role of assistant and concert organizer.

On June 15 John Hutchinson decided to leave the Buzz due to non-payments, and in the following weeks Bowie was forced to play a couple of gigs without a guitarist before hiring former Anteeeks Billy Gray. In any case, producer Tony Hatch decided to exclude what was left of the band from recording the new single *I Dig Everything*, scheduled to be released the following month, and to use some turners. The 45 was released on August 19 and turned out to be yet another commercial failure despite some encouraging reviews in the trade press, so that in September Tony Hatch and Pye released Bowie from his contract. the new manager succeeded in arousing the interest of Deram Records and producer Mike Vernon, with whom he would soon record his debut album simply titled *David Bowie*.

The new narrative direction in which Bowie's songs were moving was the source of some controversy with the Buzz: "I found it incredible that 99 percent of our live songs were soulful, and that I was writing in such a musical/vaudeville style," the singer remarked in 1999. The group ceased to exist on December 2, although it participated in the recording of the album and singles *Rubber Band* and *The Laughing Gnome*, and at the end of the year David wrote the song *Over the Wall We Go*, released in January 1967 as a single by English actor and singer Paul Nicholas. By mid-1966 David was thus a singer who had been in a handful of bands, with six unsuccessful singles under his belt and, most importantly, no contract. The only silver lining was that Kenneth Pitt was making an effort to promote his career in the right direction and succeeded in attracting the interest of Deram Records, a newly formed subsidiary of Decca for which Bowie would soon record his debut album. Together with bassist Derek Fearnley, he planned to recover some of his old tunes, and Pitt allowed them to record them with the intention of having enough material for an EP. On October 18, at R.G. Jones Studios in London *Rubber Band*, *The Gravedigger* (which would later become *Please Mr. Gravedigger*) and *The London Boys* were recorded. Both Decca's head of promotion, Tony Hall, and manager Hugh Mendl were quite impressed with the result: four days later Pitt met with producer Mike Vernon and succeeded in securing the first album for David Bowie, of which *Rubber Band* would be the first single taken.

But in the Buzz things were not going well, mainly because of the new narrative direction in which Bowie's songs were moving. The group ceased to exist on December 2 after a concert in Shrewsbury, the same day

Rubber Band was released, although Boyes, Fearnley and Eager continued to participate in *David Bowie*'s recordings (and other songs not included on the album such as *The Laughing Gnome*) until February 1967.

At the end of the year, during the album sessions David also wrote a song for English actor and singer Paul Nicholas, to which he also contributed backing vocals. What would become Oscar's (the stage name used by Nicholas) third single in June 1967 is titled *Over the Wall We Go* and speaks in a joking tone about escaped convicts and incompetent policemen.

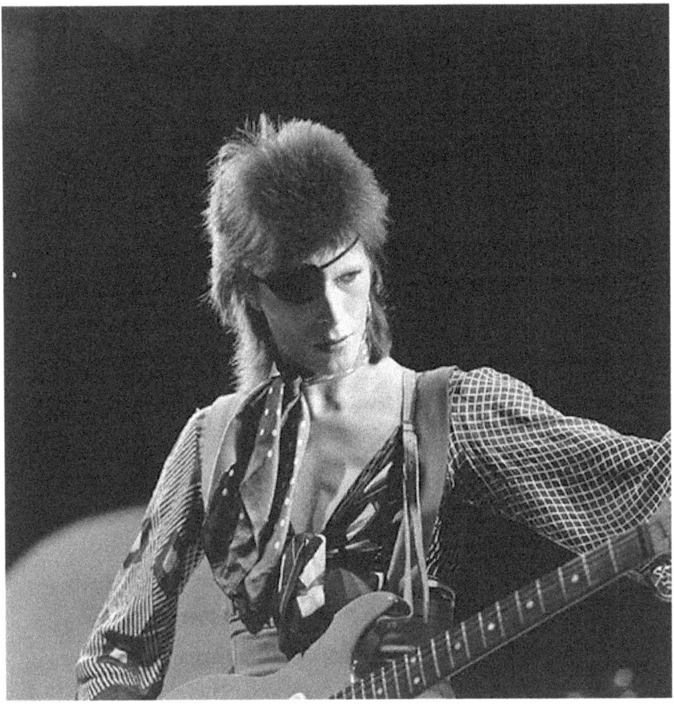

Space Oddity and early successes (1967-1969)

Increasingly oriented toward a solo career, he was briefly part of several bands in 1967 and, with the Riot Squad, recorded *Little Toy Soldier*, a sadomasochistic theme song with obvious references to *Venus in Furs* by the Velvet Underground. Lou Reed's decadent streak, however, gives way to a music-hall atmosphere enhanced by cackling, coughing, creaking springs, explosions and other noises by sound engineer and future *Space Oddity* producer Gus Dudgeon.

The following April saw the release of a new 45, *The Laughing Gnome*, described by *NME*'s Roy Carr and Charles Shaar Murray as "*undoubtedly the most embarrassing example of Bowie's iuvenalia,*" and, by biographer David Buckley, "*utterly stupid, though perversely catchy.*" Despite the poor success of the single, his first album, *David Bowie, was* released in June 1967, which had little commercial success despite receiving some positive reviews. Meanwhile, other tracks were recorded for Deram, but Deram refused to release them, partly because of the album's poor sales. Actor and mime Lindsay Kemp later stated, " [...] *I listened to it until I wore it out.*" In the fall of that year, *Let Me Sleep Beside You* and *Karma Man* were recorded. These were also not released by Deram, but the former of the two represented the beginning of one of Bowie's seminal collaborations, that with Tony Visconti, whom he met in the studios of his own publisher David Platz.

At this same time his filmmaking experience began with his participation in Michael Armstrong's short film, *The Image*; talking about it again in 1983, Bowie described it as " [...] *black-and-white underground avant-garde stuff, made by a certain guy.... He wanted to make a movie about a painter taking a portrait of a teenager, but the portrait comes to life and, basically, it turns out to be somebody's dead body. I don't really remember the plot-it was terrible.*"

After performing the new single *Love You Till Tuesday* on the Dutch television program *Fanclub* and performing at the Stage Ball in London, a dance for the charity British Heart Foundation, where he sang accompanied by the Bill Savill Orchestra, on December 18, 1967, he performed in a "BBC session" for John Peel's *Top Gear* radio program, in which Bowie was accompanied by the sixteen-piece orchestra of Arthur Greenslade. Then, on December 28, at the Oxford Playhouse, a first series of performances of the show *Pierrot in Turquoise*, centered on a love triangle between Pierrot, Columbine, and Harlequin, concluded.

The role of Cloud, played by Bowie, was that of a sort of character-narrator, whose constant changes were committed to deluding and deceiving the hapless protagonist. During the performance he played *When I Live My Dream* and *Sell Me a Coat*, along with three compositions written especially for the occasion (*Threepenny Pierrot*, *Columbine* and *The Mirror*), all accompanied on piano by Michael Garrett. The local *Oxford Mail* newspaper wrote, "*David Bowie has composed some fascinating songs, which he sings in a splendid dreamy voice*," while finding that the show as a whole "*succeeds only in hinting at the universal truths that Marcel Marceau manages to express.*"

On February 27, 1968 Bowie traveled to Hamburg to record three songs for the ZDF network's *4-3-2-1 Musik Für Junge Leute* program. Upon his return he recorded *In the Heat of the Morning* and *London Bye Ta-Ta* with Visconti, but Deram's umpteenth refusal to release prompted the singer to leave the label for good.

In the spring, performances of *Pierrot in Turquoise at the* Mercury Theatre and the Intimate Theater in London continued with some success. Bowie then recorded a second session of songs at the BBC, followed by a concert at the Middle Earth Club in Covent Garden, where he backed up T. Rex, and one at the Royal Festival Hall. In both appearances he performed the short mime piece

Jetsun and the Eagle, which gave rise to *Wild Eyed Boy from Freecloud*, inspired by the Tibetan cleric and poet Milarepa and acted with background music that included *Silly Boy Blue*.

After a fleeting appearance in *The Pistol Shot*, a BBC script based on the life of Russian poet Pushkin, Bowie went to live with partner Hermione in London's South Kensington, and began planning a *one-man show* designed specifically for the cabaret circuit by putting together a repertoire that alternated between his own songs (*When I'm Five*, *Love You Till Tuesday*, *The Laughing Gnome*, *When I Live My Dream*, *Even a Fool Learns to Love*) and Beatles covers such as *Yellow Submarine* and *All You Need Is Love*; in the summer he held two auditions to pitch his show but both were unsuccessful. He then put together the acoustic trio Turquoise with Hermione and Tony Hill, former guitarist with Misunderstood, with a repertoire that included some of his more bizarre compositions, including the unreleased *Ching-a-Ling* and a selection of covers that represented Bowie's first sortie into the work of Jacques Brel.

Bowie's first real concert was held on September 14 at the Roundhouse in London; after a few dates guitarist Tony Hill left and was replaced by John Hutchinson. Renamed Feathers, the group debuted on November 17 at the Country Club in Haverstock Hill. In addition to the songs, the trio members took turns reciting poetry while Bowie performed his mime piece *The Mask*.

While the two groups Slender Plenty and The Beatstalkers released the song Bowie had written the previous year, *Silver Tree Top School for Boys*, the last engagements of the year were both for German television: his second appearance in *4-3-2-1 Musik Für Junge Leute* and his appearance in *Für Jeden Etwas Musik*, where Bowie acted out a mime piece and sang a song.

Another important meeting for Bowie took place in early 1969, that with 19-year-old American Mary Angela Barnett, who four months later became his partner and then his wife in March 1970; but the meeting with Barnett was mainly linked to their mutual acquaintance with Calvin Mark Lee, director for Europe of the A&R division of Mercury Records in New York, whom Bowie met as early as 1967, at the meeting with general manager Simon Hayes. According to biographers Peter and Leni Gillman, it also appears that Calvin Mark Lee was involved with the singer in a relationship that went beyond mere friendship, and this would perhaps have been the "three-way relationship" to which Bowie referred many years later when he provocatively claimed in an interview that he met his future wife when "*we were both dating the same man.*"

On January 22 Bowie recorded a commercial for Lyons Maid's *Luv* ice cream, directed by Ridley Scott, and four days later began filming the video album *Love You Till Tuesday*. During this period he performed with John Hutchinson his first live performance of the year at the University of Sussex. He also participated in some Tyrannosaurus Rex tour dates, performing mime sequences, and unsuccessfully attempted an audition for the musical *Hair* at the Shaftesbury Theatre in London.

In the same days Bowie and Hutchinson abandoned mime and poetry and focused on more sophisticated folk sounds, based on twin acoustic guitars and vocal harmonies. They recorded a demo with ten acoustic pieces, which formed the basis for the new album.

Before the summer the singer and his new partner, *Sunday Times* journalist Mary Finnigan, founded a folk club at the Three Tuns pub in Beckenham and began holding weekly meetings attended by more and more intellectuals, poets, film students and other creative people. This new reality was christened *Growth*.

On June 14 Bowie and Visconti were guests of the Strawbs on the BBC's *Colour Me Pop* program, and a few days later at Trident Studios in Soho recording of the new LP began, where sound engineer Dudgeon supervised the two tracks that constituted the first 45 from the album, *Space Oddity* and *Wild Eyed Boy from Freecloud*. These sessions represented an opportunity for Bowie to play with new musicians who later worked with him again: bassist Herbie Flowers, who would also play on the 1974 album, *Diamond Dogs*, and Rick Wakeman, who participated in the making of the 1971 album, *Hunky Dory*, and Visconti himself.

Only three weeks after recording and in time for the first Apollo 11 moon landing, the *Space Oddity* 45 was released on July 11, 1969 in two different versions in both the UK and the US, with good reception from the trade press.

At the end of the month he traveled with Pitt to Valletta for the Malta Song Festival, where Bowie performed *When I Live My Dream* and the unreleased *No-One; Someone*, while a few days later there was his first performance in Italy in Monsummano Terme, for the International Record Award, where he won his first award for *When I Live My Dream*.

Recording of the album continued throughout the summer, and Visconti recruited several other musicians for the occasion as well as Rats guitarist Mick Ronson, who made his official debut with the British singer by playing a brief guitar solo on the middle section of *Wild Eyed Boy from Freecloud.* In mid-August, a free festival organized by *Growth*, Bowie's art workshop, was held at the Beckenham Recreation Ground, where the Strawbs also performed; there were about 3,000 attendees and the event was immortalized in the song *Memory of a Free Festival*, although it seems that Bowie's mood that day was at odds with the nostalgic feelings expressed in the song, perhaps because of the death of his father, who had passed away a few days earlier from pneumonia. However, the Beckenham festival represented Bowie's farewell from the hippie movement, disgusted by the mediocrity and indolence of many of its adherents, as well as the last act of the *Growth* artistic laboratory, attended essentially by apathetic spectators rather than active contributors as he had intended.

At the end of August, after recording a version of *Space Oddity* for the Dutch television program *Doebidoe*, he managed to get Pitt a contract with Mercury Records for a new record to be distributed in the UK by the Philips affiliate. The choice of producer initially fell on George Martin but then Tony Visconti was chosen.

After a live performance at Library Gardens in Bromley, in October he recorded his first appearance on the BBC program *Top of the Pops* where he performed *Space Oddity* which, in the meantime, reached #5 in the UK charts representing his first real hit. This was followed by a BBC recording with Junior's Eyes for the *Dave Lee Travis Show*. At the same time Bowie and Barnett moved to Beckenham to a building at Haddon Hall, which in later years became the unofficial recording studio, as well as a photography studio and common area for the singer's *entourage.* During this period he performed the song of the moment, *Space Oddity,* on several occasions, including Swiss television's *Hits à gogo* program and ZDF's *4-3-2-1 Musik für Junge Leute.*

An initial short Scottish tour began in November, which coincided with the release of his second album, distributed in the UK under the title *David Bowie, which* is the same title as the first LP, and in the United States as *Man of Words/Man of Music*; it was not until 1972 that it was reissued by RCA under the title *Space Oddity*, by which it was then forever known. The vinyl won the title of the most expensive record ever sold on the Discogs platform in 2016. Bowie, who played a number of tracks from the new LP alternating with some covers, did not yet have much live experience, and those few were mostly limited to amplified rhythm and blues, so he was unprepared for the cold reception given to that new acoustic style of his: " [...] I didn'*t realize what the audience was like in those days. There was a mod revival that had then morphed into the skinhead movement. They found me unbearable.*"

During this period, after having his hair cut in a military style due to his participation a few months earlier in the film *The Virgin* Soldiers in which he played the role of a soldier, he appeared with a messy curly perm, which he would continue to sport until the early 1970s.

Toward the end of 1969, he participated in a very successful concert at the Royal Festival Hall although the absence of journalists prevented the event from being publicized in the national press. Among the few who reviewed the concert was Tony Palmer of the *Observer,* who called it "*scorching*" and said *Space Oddity* was "*spectacularly beautiful*," although other performances such as *An Occasional Dream* were described by him as "*gloomy, monotonous and full of self-pity.*"

The year 1969 ended with the recording of *Ragazzo solo, ragazza sola*, the Italian version of *Space Oddity*, albeit with lyrics not related to the original, and *Hole in the Ground*, which was performed at the *Save Rave '69* benefit concert. Although the second album proved to be a commercial failure, with sales barely exceeding 5,000 copies in the UK by March 1970, Bowie was voted best emerging artist in a readers' poll by *Music Now!*, while Penny Valentine of *Disc and Music Echo* named *Space Oddity* album of the year.

Metamorphosis: from "folk" to "glam rock" (1970-1971)

Early engagements in 1970 were the recording of *The Looking Glass Murders*, a television adaptation of *Pierrot in Turquoise,* the filming of which was held at the Gateway Theatre in Edinburgh, and the recording of *The Prettiest Star*, featuring Marc Bolan on lead guitar. The careers of the two future stars, both produced by Visconti, crossed paths several times during the 1970s. Meanwhile, at a concert at the Marquee Club there was a reunion with Mick Ronson, who became Bowie's full-time guitarist, joining Visconti and Junior's Eyes drummer John Cambridge. The new group was called Hype, short for *hypocritical*, Bowie's irony about the hypocrisy surrounding the alternative music world. "I deliberately chose that name because I wanted something that sounded a little strong, so now no one can say they were misled," Bowie would tell *Melody Maker*. The new quartet debuted at the BBC sessions the following February. Soon after, the Hype made their concert debut at London's Roundhouse, and here, after months of personal experiments with costumes and makeup, the metamorphosis took place: Bowie forced the group to wear the extravagant outfits sewn by Visconti's wife and girlfriend. Each member also assumed the identity of a comic book character, and Bowie, in multicolored lurex stockings, high boots and a blue cape, became "Rainbowman." The concert is considered the birth act of glam rock, but the audience's reception was cold; the members of the Hype themselves appeared skeptical, except for Bowie who seemed to have no doubts: " [...] after that concert I stopped, I didn't experiment with other things because I knew it was okay," he recounted in *NME* a few years later, " [...] I knew very well what I wanted to do and I was sure that many others would too. But I was going to be the first."

Soon after, Bowie returned to Scotland, host of Grampian TV's *Cairngorm Ski Night* program; accompanied by a large television orchestra he performed *London Bye Ta-Ta* and performed a dance number with Angela and Lindsay Kemp.Meanwhile, Visconti and Ronson set up a recording studio at Haddon Hall, where much of the material from this period was made. Frequent visits to the studio were made by Terry Burns, Bowie's half-brother, who, though a voluntary resident at Cane Hill Hospital, often hung out with the group.These frequent visits had a major influence on some of the compositions that ended up on the new album.

Later the 45 rpm *The Prettiest Star* was released, a true declaration of love to Barnett, receiving considerable attention from British music magazines since it was released after the success of *Space Oddity.* However, the good press reception was not matched commercially, and the single did not exceed 800 copies sold. For the American market, Mercury Records preferred instead to focus on a new, more concise and energetic recording of *Memory of a Free Festival*, but the operation proved a failure.

On March 20, 1970, David Bowie and Angela Barnett were married in Bromley Town Hall, in an informal ceremony attended by a few friends and Bowie's mother. Five days later the Hype recorded another session at the BBC for the Andy Ferris show, after which they disbanded and the group held their last concert at the Star Hotel in Croydon. During that time Angela worked hard to help David, such as keeping in touch with *promoters* and generally taking care of public relations, booking the halls where her husband was to perform, controlling lighting and sound for concerts, etc. She would also contribute to her husband's new androgynous image by, among other things, advising him on the choice of costumes, hairstyles and attitudes to be held in public.

Bowie then continued to perform live as a solo artist, offering mainly tracks from *Space Oddity* but also previews of tracks that ended up on later albums. During this period he also recorded the unreleased track *Tired of my life*, which some sources say Bowie wrote when he was 16 years old, and *The World of David Bowie*, the first official collection containing tracks from the debut album and some previously unreleased tracks, was released. Recording sessions for *The Man Who Sold the World* began from April 18 to May 22 at Trident Studios. Cambridge was replaced on drums by Mick "Woody" Woodmansey, Ronson's former colleague in the Rats, while Visconti spent most of the sessions trying to stimulate the newlywed, fighting against his apparent apathy for the project. The group's elements became five with the arrival of keyboardist Ralph Mace, a Philips Records executive who became Bowie's reference within the label earlier that year during the recording of *The Prettiest Star*.

Once the recordings were finished, Bowie's activities slowed down and, unhappy with the direction Pitt tried to give his work, he showed up with young legal adviser Tony Defries at the manager's home, who agreed to dissolve all professional obligations. The two parted amicably, and Defries became the artist's full-time manager. Pitt remained, however, one of the most influential figures of the British singer's early period, with considerable personal investment, although considerably less than the funds made available by Defries' colleague

Laurence Myers, with whom he had just created the Gem Music Group; his last engagement with Pitt was the Ivor Novello Awards ceremony, held on May 10 at Talk Of the Town in London: Bowie sang *Space Oddity* and won an award. The song was performed with an extensive orchestral arrangement arranged by Paul Buckmaster and conducted by Les Reed, and the performance was broadcast via satellite in Europe and the United States, while in England it was broadcast only on radio.

In the meantime, the success achieved the year before with the same song wore off, and so in October Defries negotiated an offer with Chrysalis Records, managing to secure a deal and a £5,000 advance, while Bowie channeled his energies into a period of intensive writing. On November 4, 1970, *The Man Who Sold the World* was released in the United States and received a good critical reception despite poor sales. Ronson's hard rock guitar was a conspicuous change from the predominantly folk and acoustic atmospheres of the previous album. The lyrics appeared more complex and less linear than before, and the deeper themes addressed would be echoed in Bowie's later works: sexual ambiguity, split personalities, isolation, madness, false gurus, totalitarianism. Bowie soon thought about the next album. Bob Grace, general manager of Chrysalis, rented the London studios of Radio Luxembourg where the singer began recording new material, including the song *Oh! You Pretty Things*.

The following year the new 45 was released, *Holy Holy*, despite a six-month delay in recording caused by contract negotiations. A few days later the song was performed on Granada TV's *Six-O-One: Newsday* program, but without success. 1971 represented a crucial moment for Bowie's career, in which Defries was instrumental in realizing and promoting the ideas birthed by the singer's genius; the manager was radically revolutionizing the entire organization that had marked his career up to that point and convinced him to sever his relationship with Tony Visconti, who was guilty of maintaining relations with Marc Bolan, who at that point was contending for Bowie's role as the prima donna of glam rock. Visconti left and concentrated on producing Marc Bolan and T. Rex, keeping the Hype name and hiring Rats singer Benny Marshall to join Ronson and Woodmansey. He would resume his collaboration with Bowie in 1974, when relations between the singer and Defries were deteriorating.

In February Bowie embarked on his first trip to the United States for the short promotional tour of *The Man Who Sold the World*. Although his marriage to Angela had enabled him to obtain a *green card*, Bowie could not perform because of union agreements with the American Federation of Musicians, and promotion was limited to personal appearances and a few interviews in Washington, New York, Chicago, Philadelphia, San

Francisco, and Los Angeles. In one of these interviews he announced to John Mendelsohn of *Rolling Stone* that he wanted to "introduce mime in a traditional Western setting, to attract the audience's attention with a series of very stylized, very Japanese movements." On the same occasion he also declared that rock music "should be dressed up as a prostitute, as a parody of itself, it should be a kind of clown, of Pierrot. The music is the mask that hides the message. The music is the Pierrot and I, the artist, am the message."

After this brief American interlude Bowie returned to Trident Studios to complete the new album *Hunky Dory*, making new songs including *Changes* and *Life on Mars?* Among the instrumentalists initially employed were some Dulwich students who had given themselves the name Runk, including guitarist Mark Carr Pritchard, who was in the Arnold Corns, bassist Polak de Somogyl and drummer Ralph St. Laurent Broadbent. Other musicians with whom he had collaborated in previous months including Terry Cox, the drummer of *Space Oddity*, and Tony Hill, whom Bowie had known since 1968, were also considered for subsequent recordings.

The album *The Man Who Sold the World* also saw the light of day in Britain almost a year after the end of recording, but despite favorable reviews, just as had happened overseas, sales were disastrous. Bowie's contract with

Mercury was about to expire, but the company would still be willing to renew it for another album. The following month, record company representative Robin McBride arrived in London from Chicago to offer him a new three-year contract. Defries replied that if Mercury exercised the renewal option to get a new record, they would hand him "the biggest piece of crap they ever had," informing him that under no circumstances would Bowie record another note with Mercury, which agreed to terminate the contract.

Bowie was preparing material for the new album at a breakneck pace and recalled Ronson and Woodmansey; Ronson agreed and brought in bassist Trevor Bolder to replace Visconti. Thus the lineup of the future Spiders from Mars began to be outlined.

The band moved to Haddon Hall to rehearse new compositions, and Bowie decided to use the upcoming session at the BBC on June 3 as a showcase for his renewed circle of musicians, including friends Dana Gillespie, George Underwood, and Geoffrey Alexander, to perform some new songs including *Kooks*, composed for his son Zowie. On June 23 Bowie attended the Glastonbury Fayre during which Hawkwind, Traffic, Joan Baez and Pink Floyd, among others, performed. The previous night's set list had been stretched out of proportion and Bowie's concert had been canceled because authorities insisted on ending the event by 10:30 p.m.; undaunted, Bowie began playing at 5 a.m. with some inconvenience that interrupted *Oh! You Pretty Things* and continued with six more songs including *Memory of a Free Festival*.

The recording of *Hunky Dory* continued at Trident Studios throughout the summer, and in August Defries flew to New York with 500 promotional copies of a vinyl called *BOWPROMO 1A1/1B1*, with songs by Dana Gillespie on one side and some new Bowie recordings on the other, including *Andy Warhol*, *Queen Bitch,* and the unreleased *Bombers.* After a few days the manager returned with a contract with RCA.

During the last phase of the making of *Hunky Dory* another crucial element for Bowie's future career appeared. In the summer of 1971 the U.S. production entitled *Pork*, an Andy Warhol adaptation of a collection of conversations recorded in New York City's equivocal circles, was staged at the Roundhouse in London, bringing together the transvestite Wayne County, the uninhibited Geri Miller and Cherry Vanilla with Tony Zanetta playing Warhol himself. To the British public, *Pork*'s scenes of masturbation, homosexuality, drugs and abortions represented an unacceptable affront to good taste. The show received immense free publicity from the scandalized comments of the press, while for Bowie, contact with Warhol's bizarreness represented a new turning point. This event and the meeting with the American artist that took place the following month contributed to his insight into the fusion of music and staging, changing his own *look* and exploiting the *media* to create his new rock-star image. His role on stage was no longer limited to that of singer-musician with good use of body movements, but that of actor-musician.

Attracted by their brashness, murky sexuality, typically New York street style, and ties to Warhol, Bowie hastened to introduce the members of the new cast to Defries upon his return from the United States. When Defries exited the Gem Music Group in 1972 and founded MainMan Management, a company he wholly owned with which he managed the enormous amount of business that Bowie would be able to move, some of *Pork*'s key players were hired and had prominent roles in the company.

Having finished recording *Hunky Dory*, Bowie returned to America with Angela, Defries and Ronson to sign the new contract with RCA. As with his previous trip, Bowie was unable to perform, but his stay allowed him to meet Warhol personally, to whom he played the song dedicated to him. As Bowie revealed in 1997, Warhol did not have a positive reaction: " [...] I think he thought he was humiliated by the song or something and really that was not my intention, in fact, it was an ironic homage. He took it very badly but he liked my shoes.... I was wearing a pair that Marc Bolan had given me, bright canary yellow, with a heel and a rounded toe [...] since Warhol also had a habit of designing shoes, we had something to talk about." Two other important encounters took place in the same days: Dennis Katz of RCA introduced him to Lou Reed at a restaurant, and the same night, at a party at Max's Kansas City, he met Iggy Pop, an encounter that would prove pivotal to both of their careers in the future.

Upon returning to Europe, Bowie's live and studio engagements continued, with recordings of *The Rise and Fall of Ziggy Stardust and the Spiders from Mars* beginning on September 9 with a cover of *It Ain't Easy* by U.S. singer-songwriter Ron Davies. On September 21 there was a new session at the BBC for *Sounds of the 70s* with "Whispering" Bob Harris, in which Bowie and Ronson played Brel's *Amsterdam*. Four days later there was the first live performance with the future Spiders from Mars, with the addition of Tom Parker on piano, at the Friars Club in Aylesbury.

On November 8, the first real session began, which produced many of the tracks destined for the new album. These included new versions of *Moonage Daydream* and *Hang On to Yourself*, the famous *Ziggy Stardust* and *Lady Stardust*; the last two had already been recorded in an acoustic demo at Radio Luxembourg studios a few months earlier. Among the discarded tracks were *Shadow Man*, *Sweet Head*, *Velvet Goldmine*, a new version of *Holy Holy,* and a rendition of Chuck Berry's *Around and Around,* re-titled *Round and Round*.

Hunky Dory was released on December 17, 1971, when Bowie was already halfway through recording his next album and working on another change of image and style. The new work saw a return to more folk sounds dominated by Rick Wakeman's piano and Mick Ronson's operatic arrangements and, above all, showcased Bowie's acquired skill as a songwriter but, despite glowing reviews in the trade press and the release of the single *Changes*, the promotional campaign was inadequate and sales poor. In the United States it stopped at position No. 93 on the Billboard 200 while in the United Kingdom one even had to wait for the release of *Ziggy Stardust* to see it on the charts. *Hunky Dory* was nevertheless considered through the years to be his first, authentic "classic" album.

The Age of Ziggy Stardust (1972-1973)

The real consecration came in 1972, with the album *The Rise and Fall of Ziggy Stardust and the Spiders from Mars*, in which he was accompanied by the eponymous band The Spiders from Mars and which contains most of his classics, which continued to be repeated in any of his concerts even thirty years later: from *Starman* to *Moonage Daydream*, from *Rock 'n' Roll Suicide* to *Ziggy Stardust* In the same year, to introduce his first major hitSpace *Oddity*(1969) to the American market, Bowie performed the song in his first video clip, filmed at RCA studios in New York.

Between 1972 and 1973, he took on tour a show where the real Bowie and the Ziggy Stardust character ended up blending together. Dressed in tight, colorful tights, garish costumes, and hair dyed fiery red, Bowie kicked off the first Ziggy show in the intimate setting of Tolworth's Toby Jug Pub on February 10, 1972. The show, which was later presented to larger audiences, permanently catapulted Bowie into the British media spotlight over the next six months of touring, earning him enormous popularity and growing acclaim from audiences and critics alike. Crowds of young boys and girls flocked to his concerts impressed by the lashing, melodic glam rock and the attitude of sexual freedom that shone through from the ephebe Ziggy. *The Rise and Fall of Ziggy Stardust and the Spiders from Mars*, combining the hard rock elements of *The Man Who Sold the World* with the more pop and experimental approach of *Hunky Dory*, was released in June 1972: it reached No. 5 in the UK and stayed on the charts for about two years while also pulling the previous *Hunky Dory*, now six months old, back into the charts to success. This success was due in large part to Bowie's appearance on Top of the Pops, where he had presented the single (taken from the new album) Starman, which in turn reached number 10 on the charts. Also released within a few weeks were the single *John, I'm Only Dancing*, not contained on the album, and *All the Young Dudes*, a song written and produced for Mott the Hoople, which became hits in the UK. The Ziggy Stardust Tour continued in the United States of America.

During this period, Bowie contributed as producer and musician, along with Ronson, to the biggest commercial success of Lou Reed's career, the album *Transformer*, considered a milestone of glam rock.

The next studio work was the album *Aladdin Sane*, which became Bowie's first album to reach the top of the British charts. Described by Bowie himself as "Ziggy Goes to

America," to emphasize the Americanization of the glam sound of the previous year, the album contains songs written while traveling across the United States for the first dates of the Ziggy Tour, which continued to Japan. Two hit singles were extracted from *Aladdin Sane, which* reached the top of the British charts, *The Jean Genie* and *Drive-In Saturday*.

The title stems from the play on words reflecting Bowie's dual personality at the time: on one side the supernatural and wholesome Aladdin *(Aladdin Sane)* and on the other the insane boy *(A lad insane)*. Famous became the record's iconic cover image, a half-length photo of Bowie in Aladdin Sane makeup, with a red lightning bolt across his face, one of the most recognizable and emblematic depictions of the artist over the decades.

Bowie's love of acting and theatricality led him to total immersion in his androgynous musical alter ego. In retrospect, the musician stated, "Onstage I was a robot while offstage I felt emotions instead. That's probably why I preferred dressing up as Ziggy rather than being David." With success came personal difficulties, however: playing the same role over and over again made it increasingly difficult for Bowie to separate his characters from his true personality; "Ziggy," Bowie said, "would not leave me for years. That was the point where everything went too far [...] . My whole personality was affected. It became very dangerous. I began to seriously doubt my sanity."

Ziggy's last concerts, which included songs from both *Ziggy Stardust* and *Aladdin Sane*, were utterly theatrical and included studied moments of onstage pathos alternating with disconcerting gestures, with Bowie simulating fellatio with Ronson's guitar. The artist ended this period with the dramatic announcement of his retirement from the stage as the character Ziggy during a concert at London's Hammersmith Odeon on July 3, 1973, right at the height of his success.

After disbanding the Spiders from Mars, Bowie tried to move away from the Ziggy persona for good. Confirming the great success of the moment, all the albums in his past catalog also sold well: *The Man Who Sold the World* was reissued in 1972 along with *Space Oddity*. The song *Life on Mars?* was released as a single in June 1973 and reached number three on the UK charts. *Pin Ups*, a collection of covers of Bowie's favorite 1960s songs, was released in October, reaching No. 1 on the UK charts. By 1973 there were six Bowie albums on the UK charts, and commercial success, at least in his homeland, had been largely achieved.

Toward the end of the year Bowie intertwined an intense but brief liaison with Amanda Lear, whom he discovered upon seeing her on the cover of Roxy Music's *For Your*

Pleasure album. It was Bowie himself who convinced her to give up modeling to embrace a singing career, even financing some singing and dance classes for her.

Funk, "plastic soul" and *Diamond Dogs* (1974-1975)

In March 1974 Bowie boarded the ocean liner SS France, reaching the United States on April 1, initially settling in New York City.

The Diamond Dogs album of the same year was the result of two different ideas: an aborted musical based on the apocalyptic future described in George Orwell's novel *1984* and the early soul and funk influences that began to creep into Bowie's music.

With hit tracks such as *Rebel Rebel* and *Diamond Dogs*, the record became number one in Britain and number five in the United States. To promote it, Bowie kicked off the spectacular *Diamond Dogs Tour*, attending major cities in North America between June and December 1974. The heavily staged and theatrical tour coincided with the singer's increasing cocaine addiction, which caused him a variety of physical problems due to debilitation. In April 1975 he moved to California, to a house in the hills of Los Angeles; here Bowie spent one of the most negative periods of his life, obsessed with his passion for occultism and debilitated by heavy drug abuse. However, this dark period contributed in part to the birth of his next persona.

Bowie himself, given his precarious state of health, commented on the next live album, *David Live*, ironically saying that it should have been titled "*David Bowie is alive and well but living only in theory.*" Nevertheless, *David Live* solidified Bowie's status as a rock star, reaching number two in England and number eight in the United States. After a break in Philadelphia, where Bowie recorded new material, the tour continued with more emphasis on soul music, the singer's last great passion.

The fruit of the sessions in Philadelphia was the album *Young Americans* released in 1975, in which the artist, having finally shed his colorful glam rock hero shoes, threw himself headlong into American black music. Biographer Christopher Sandford wrote, " [...] over the years, many British musicians had tried to become "black" by aping American black music but few had succeeded as successfully as Bowie."

The album's distinctive and contrived sound, which Bowie himself described as "plastic soul," constituted a radical new turn in his musical style. From *Young Americans* was extracted the single *Fame*, composed with John Lennon and Carlos Alomar, which earned Bowie the top spot on the charts, for two weeks, in the United States. The album marked an important phase in the artist's musical evolution: it was the first of his albums to almost completely abandon rock in favor of more funky and soulful sounds, giving rise to a kind of "white R&B."

That was when the relationship between Defries and Bowie ended; he had been superficial in signing the contract with MainMan, had not read it carefully, and had trusted what Defries had told him. Convinced that he was 50 percent co-owner of the company and entitled to half of the earnings, he was not informed until 1974 that the company was 100 percent Defries'. The contract provided for 50 percent of the gross revenues to Defries and 50 percent to Bowie, but Bowie had to shoulder the entirety of the very large expenses and taxes.

When Bowie learned such details, MainMan was burdened with debt, both in the U.K. and the U.S. Many bills had not been paid and expenses had risen, along with Defries' misguided investments. Bowie felt betrayed and exploited; his first reaction was to cut the exorbitant concert expenses and adopt more sober costumes and settings, renaming the tour the "Philly Dogs Tour." On Jan. 29, 1975, he went to the RCA offices and announced his departure from MainMan, getting an advance for *Young Americans* soon to be released. The next day the contract termination letter arrived at MainMan.

After the contract was terminated in 1975, Bowie would claim that he was treated like a slave by Defries and failed to make money. Negotiations to terminate the contract were long and difficult, and eventually Bowie was forced to pay Defries 50 percent of the *royalties* on the works made by *Hunky Dory* up to that point and 16 percent on those of all his own work up to 1982. Defries continued to retain a portion of the copyright on Bowie's records until 1997, when the singer redeemed the former manager's shares and became 100 percent owner of those rights. Bowie's new manager and his attorney was briefly Michael Lippman.

The "White Duke" years and the Berlin trilogy (1976-1979)

The release of the subsequent album *Station to Station* in January 1976 was followed in February by a three-and-a-half-month tour of Europe and the United States to promote the album and the dramatic performances of Bowie's new persona, the *thin* White Duke.

This new alter ego marked one of many artistic turning points in his career, now far removed from the boisterous multicolored glam rock clamor of a few years earlier. The "White Duke" impersonated an aristocratic character with understated and elegant attire, hypothetical right-wing sympathies, and a strong infatuation with occultism. Although many of these elements were merely stage gimmicks of the multifaceted artist, the name "White Duke" entered the public's collective imagination and soon became his more customary nickname for the rest of his career.

The most significant songs of this period were the album's *title track*, influenced by the sound of German krautrock groups, the ballads *Word on a Wing* and *Wild Is the Wind*, a cover of a song made famous by Nina Simone, and the funky tracks *TVC 15* and *Stay*. The band that accompanied Bowie onstage included guitarist Carlos Alomar, bassist George Murray, and drummer Dennis Davis, a rhythm section that would accompany him until the end of the decade. The tour was a great success but also generated political controversy, such as the one that arose during a date in Stockholm, in which Bowie was accused of making the following statement: " [...] Britain would benefit from the advent of a fascist leader [...]"; also shortly thereafter, border police stopped him on the Polish-Russian border for possession of some Nazi memorabilia.

The controversial affair culminated in London the following May in what became known as "the Victoria Station incident." On the afternoon of May 2, 1976, back in Britain after a two-year absence, Bowie left the station waving to the crowd of adoring fans with a left arm gesture that was mistaken for a Nazi salute, an incident that was photographed and published in *NME*. Bowie stated that the photographer had simply "frozen" the gesture of his arm in midair in the course of a normal salute. Most of the British press ignored the incident, however, the various tabloid tabloids speculated in no small part about the singer's alleged Nazi tendencies, fueling it with recycled quotes from previous years, such as one given by Bowie in an interview with Cameron

Crowe where he stated that "Adolf Hitler was one of the first real rock stars [...]," or quoting the song *Somebody Up There Likes Me* contained in the album *Young Americans,* in which he spoke of Hitler's return. Bowie later publicly apologized for these ambiguous attitudes, blaming them on his cocaine addiction and over-identification with the character of the "White Duke":" [...] I was out of my mind, totally crazy. I was mainly interested in the mythology more than the whole thing about Hitler and totalitarianism [...]."

During this period, Bowie also had his first real experience in film acting as the lead in the science fiction film *The Man Who Fell to Earth* by Nicolas Roeg, a director who cast him after liking him in the documentary *Cracked Actor* inherent in the Diamond Dogs Tour of the previous year. For the occasion, David also began composing some instrumental tracks that were supposed to form the film's soundtrack but instead flowed into his subsequent record releases.

In 1976 Bowie moved to Switzerland, buying a large villa in Blonay, in the hills near Montreaux on Lake Geneva, where his cocaine use further increased, seriously threatening his health. Determined to get sober and to distract himself from the stress of the musical environment, Bowie began painting, producing a variety of post-modernist works. He also got into the habit of taking a sketch pad on tour to draw when he felt inspired and began to photograph whatever struck his imagination. His interest in painting grew significantly enough to visit major European exhibitions and he also visited many art galleries in Geneva, the Brücke-Museum in Berlin, and became, in the words of biographer Christopher Sandford, "a prolific producer and collector of contemporary art"; his paintings were shown in many solo exhibitions and some purchased by British and U.S. museums. Through his own website Bowieart.com, he also engaged in promoting and fostering the visibility of works by young artists.

Before the end of 1976, Bowie's interest in the German art scene led him to move to West Berlin to permanently detoxify and revitalize his career. There he began a fruitful collaboration with Brian Eno and shared an apartment in Schöneberg with Iggy Pop and Corinne Schwab, his personal assistant already in Los Angeles, to whom he had entrusted most of the organizational and managerial aspects.

Schwab was the object of great jealousy from Bowie's wife Angie, who after spending a few days in Berlin moved back to the United States. Bowie dedicated to her the song *Be My Wife* included on the album *Low*, inviting her in vain to stay with him on this new adventure. The marriage had been on the rocks since 1973, with sexual passion between the two fading and frequent extra-marital affairs by both. Later, Angie would claim that she no longer wanted to see her husband after the recurrence of pro-Nazi incidents such as the Victoria Station incident. Instead, Bowie claimed that since 1974 they had been seeing each other occasionally and living separate lives. A final separation and divorce in 1980 followed.

David began to focus on minimalism and ambient music, which would characterize the albums of the so-called "*Berlin Trilogy.*" During this period he also helped lift the fortunes of Iggy Pop's career, producing and co-writing his first solo album *The Idiot* and the subsequent *Lust for Life*. On Iggy Pop's tour of Europe and the United States in March and April 1977, Bowie participated as keyboardist.

The 1977 album *Low* was partially influenced by the krautrock of Kraftwerk and Neu! and highlighted a step forward for Bowie as a composer and conceptual artist, distancing himself from simple pop and rock to produce ambitious, more abstract music where lyrics were sporadic and not essential. Despite the initial negative criticism it received for its apparent complexity and unmarketability, *Low reached number* two in the UK charts, also producing the hit single *Sound and Vision,* which itself reached number three in the UK charts.In retrospect, it would prove to be a cult album and lead avant-garde composers such as Philip Glass to describe it as " [...] a brilliant work of incomparable beauty." Glass himself will compose an entire symphony based on the album's music and atmosphere, the 1992 *Low Symphony*.

Following *Low*'s minimalist approach, *"Heroes"* was released on September 23, 1977, which includes the famous song of the same name co-written with Brian Eno; this album fused pop and rock by expanding their genre boundaries and was the only one of the three Berlin Trilogy albums to be recorded entirely in Berlin. Like *Low*, *"Heroes"* turned out to be pervaded by the Cold War *zeitgeist*, stymied by the wall that bisected the city. It was another big hit, reaching number three in the UK charts. The *title track, which* reached only #24 on the UK singles chart at the time, became perhaps the most famous and iconic song of Bowie's entire career, able to endure over the years as his signature song.Toward the end of the year, Bowie performed the track on both Marc Bolan's TV show and Bing Crosby's Christmas TV special, with whom he performed a version of *Peace on Earth/Little Drummer Boy*. The duet proved to be a worldwide hit in 1982, reaching No. 3 in the United Kingdom.

After completing *Low* and *"Heroes,"* Bowie promoted the two albums by spending most of 1978 on a tour attended by one million people in the 70 concerts that touched 12 countries. From the tour came the live album *Stage*, released the same year. Also in '78 the film *Just a Gigolo* was released, starring Bowie in the title role. The film received a mediocre audience response and poor reviews from critics.

The final chapter of the trilogy was the 1979 album *Lodger*, which in turn showed an approach to the minimalist, ambient and complex music of the previous two records but with a partial return to conventional rock based on percussion and guitars. The result was a complex mix of new wave and world music elements, with some multi-ethnic influences; some tracks were composed using aphorisms from Brian Eno and Peter Schmidt's Oblique Strategies: *Boys Keep Swinging* was born this way, encouraging the musicians to "beat" their instruments, while for *Move On* they used the chord progression of *All the Young Dudes* played backwards and for *Red Money* using the basic instrumental track of *Sister Midnight*, a song previously composed with Iggy Pop.The album was recorded entirely in Bowie's private studio in Switzerland and marked the temporary break in the collaborative relationship between Bowie and Brian Eno, who would return to work together in the 1990s. *Lodger* reached number four in Britain and number 20 in the United States, and the singles *Boys Keep Swinging* and *DJ* were extracted from the record. Although it was initially received as a minor closure to the Berlin trilogy, *Lodger* would be reevaluated over the years, partly because of the disappointing performance of Bowie's 1980s albums.

Commercial and mass success (1980-1989)

In the 1980s Bowie was heavily involved in film and theater and increased the number of stages and grandeur of tours, while record production was based on a refined yet generic pop, with albums containing some more commercial *hits*, suitable for massive radio airplay. The success of these singles was fueled by the evocative videos that accompanied them; a phenomenon, that of videos, that Bowie was already familiar with and that he exploited in the best way, as the multifaceted artist he has always proved to be.The 1980 album *Scary Monsters (and Super Creeps) was a* great success, reaching number one in the UK, thanks in part to guitar contributions from Robert Fripp, Pete Townshend, and Tom Verlaine. It produced the *chart-topping* hit *Ashes to Ashes*, which gave international visibility to the New Romantic movement, when to make its video clip Bowie recruited several extras, including Steve Strange of Visage, at the "Blitz" nightclub in London. In the video Bowie is dressed as a creepy Pierrot, in one of his most famous disguises. In September 1980 Bowie made his Broadway debut in the play *The Elephant Man* playing the part of the deformed

John Merrick, without the aid of any make-up and receiving flattering reviews.

The same year he made an appearance in the German film *Christiane F. - Us, the Berlin Zoo Boys,* whose soundtrack, composed exclusively of his tracks from *Station to Station*, *Low*, *Heroes*, and *Lodger*, was released a few months later and was a success. In 1981 Bowie collaborated with Queen on their album *Hot Space*, duetting on the track *Under Pressure* with Freddie Mercury. The track proved to be a big hit, becoming Bowie's third No. 1 single in the UK. In 1982 he starred in the BBC television adaptation of Bertolt Brecht's play *Baal*. Five of the tracks from the play, recorded in Berlin, were released on the EP of the same name.Hugely successful was the 1983 album *Let's Dance*, co-produced with Nile Rodgers of Chic, which went platinum on both sides of the Atlantic. The *title track Let's Dance*, *Modern Love,* and *China Girl were released, which* reached the top of the charts worldwide and were accompanied by acclaimed video clips that represented well the aesthetic of the 1980s.The release of *Let's Dance* was followed by the Serious Moonlight Tour, featuring guitarist Earl Slick and backing vocalists Frank and George Simms. The world tour lasted six months and was a huge success, although some critics pointed out that Bowie's music had suffered too much of a "commercial" setback.During the tour he performed with a new *look* of hyper-oxygenated hair and tanned physique, offering accessible dance-rock not without passages with disturbing themes and committed lyrics.

Also in 1983 Bowie starred in the film *Furyo*, also known by its original title *Merry Christmas Mr. Lawrence*, directed by Nagisa Ōshima and based on the novel *The Seed and the Sower* by Laurens van der Post. His performance was praised by critics, and the film was well received by audiences. 1984 saw the release of *Tonight*, another dance-oriented and highly commercial album that reached No. 1 in the UK, on which Tina Turner and Iggy Pop collaborated. Among the album's various covers was a highly criticized version of the Beach Boys' 1966 classic *God Only Knows*. There was, however, the hit *Blue Jean*, which would be featured in the short music film *Jazzin' for Blue Jean that* won the Grammy Award for Best Short Form Music Video.

In 1985 Bowie performed at Live Aid at the old Wembley Stadium in London. During the event a specially made video was shown where Bowie duets with Mick Jagger on the song *Dancing in the Street*, which later reached number one on the charts. He later starred in *Absolute Beginners* and *Labyrinth - Where Everything is Possible*, films released in 1986 for which he also curated the soundtrack. The single *Absolute Beginners* reached number two in the UK and number one on the European

Eurochart Hot 100 Singles chart. In 1987 he released the album *Never Let Me Down*, which was judged by critics to be a drab and commercial effort but was a chart success helped also by the new world tour, the mammoth and theatrical Glass Spider Tour.

The short period with the Tin Machine (1989-1990)

In 1989 he took part as singer, guitarist and saxophonist in the rock group Tin Machine, formed together with Reeves Gabrels and brothers Tony and Hunt Sales, with whom he had already collaborated in the 1970s on Iggy Pop's album *Lust for Life*; he also played keyboards on the tour documented by the live album *Tv Eye* (1978).

Although absolute democracy prevailed within Tin Machine, soon Bowie's leadership nature began to prevail in the group dynamics, both as composer and leader. In 1989, the band's debut album, *Tin Machine*, was well received by audiences and critics alike, although the over-politicization of the lyrics caused some misgivings. The record reached number three in the UK charts, and the band's first world tour proved successful. However, after a series of unsuccessful singles and a falling out with EMI, Bowie left the record label and the group disbanded after the release of a second studio album and a live album both poorly received by audiences and critics. Bowie had already returned, prior to the release of the group's second album, to solo activity with the 1990 *Sound+Vision Tour,* which kept him busy for seven months in taking his old hits around the world, following the release of the *"Sound and Vision"* box set, garnering excellent acclaim and lavish earnings. A third Tin Machine studio album had been planned, but Bowie preferred to return to solo activism after reuniting with Nile Rodgers (the producer of *Let's Dance*). With Rodgers he recorded *Real Cool World*, title track of the *Cool World* movie soundtrack, which was released as a single in the summer of 1992.

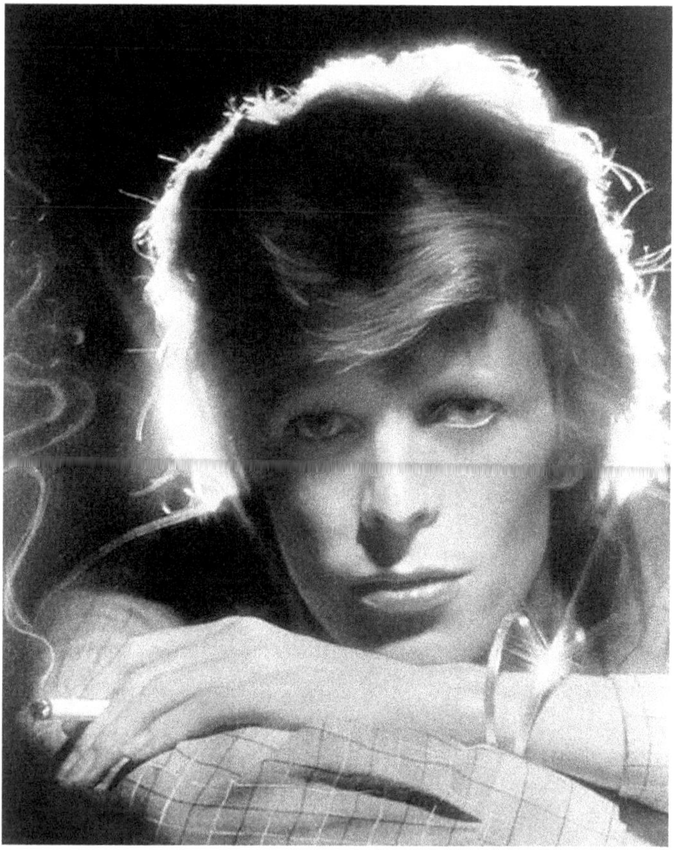

New experiments and the return to the past (1990-1999)

In 1990 he moved permanently to New York to an apartment at 160 Central Park South, on the ninth floor of the Essex House, overlooking Central Park, and devoted himself to experimentation by designing new albums, all very different from each other, which were released in the early 1990s. He also returned to the collaboration of Nile Rodgers and Brian Eno for their realization, exploring genres and musical trends of the period such as hip hop, jungle and drum and bass. Also in New York he founded Isolar Enterprises, a company to manage his song catalog, copyrights, properties and all press office activities.

In April 1992 she appeared at the Freddie Mercury Tribute Concert where she performed *Heroes*, *All the Young Dudes* and, together with Annie Lennox, *Under Pressure*. On June 6, 1992, she married Iman Mohamed Abdulmajid in a private ceremony held at St. James American Episcopal Church in Florence, Italy.

In 1993 he released the album *Black Tie White Noise*, with soul, jazz, and hip hop influences and featuring extensive use of electronic instruments; the album, produced by Nile Rodgers, reached the top of the UK charts and two singles entered the Top 40 and one the Top 10, namely the song *Jump They Say* dedicated to his half-brother Terry. Bowie later explored new *ambient* musical trends with *The Buddha of Suburbia*, the soundtrack to the TV mini-series of the same name; the album received good reviews but was a commercial failure, stopping at position No. 87 on the UK charts.

From the collaboration with Brian Eno came *1. Outside*, a concept album for which he creates new alter egos, the detective Nathan Adler, and others each assigned to interpret the tracks, thus developing the narrative of the story. Denigrated and exalted in equal measure, but in recent years reevaluated very positively, the album met with acclaim in both America and Europe and also produced some of the most successful singles of the period such as the song *Hallo Spaceboy*, later performed with the Pet Shop Boys. The album was to be part of a trilogy, but the project was shelved after the Outside Tour ended in July 1996.

On January 17, 1996, Bowie was inducted into the Rock and Roll Hall of Fame, an accolade to which was added the famous star on the Hollywood Walk of Fame, laid in

February 1997. In December 1996 Bowie became the first publicly traded rock star, offering investors bonds placed on the Wall Street exchange. The *Bowie Bonds* were valid for ten years, were secured primarily by the proceeds of 287 songs contained on his 25 albums recorded before 1990, with a total value of $55 million, and were fully purchased by the Prudential Insurance Company of New York. This transaction made Bowie one of the richest singers in the world, and his example was soon followed by artists such as Elton John, James Brown, Ashford & Simpson, and The Isley Brothers.

At the same time Bowie sensed the great potential of the web and, in addition to his personal website www.davidbowie.com, in the spring of 1996 he inaugurated *BowieNet*, the first thematic portal created by a singer, through which it was possible to connect to the web but also to legally download his music. later *BowieNet* was nominated for the 1999 Wired Award as the best entertainment site of the year and remained active until 2012.

In 1997 the new album *Earthling was* released, which included new experiments in jungle and drum and bass music; it was a success more with the public than with critics and produced the hit *Little Wonder*, a song with which he also performed at the 47th Sanremo Festival as a guest. In 1999 on the new album *'hours...'*, Bowie changed his *look* again, abandoning his short auburn hair in favor of a "hairy" *look* similar to that of his early days. The album, featuring the hit single *Thursday's Child*, has been called by *Rolling Stone* a synthesis of Bowie's career, in which his fans can find traces of earlier albums such as *Hunky Dory*, *Ziggy Stardust*, *Aladdin Sane*, *Heroes* and *Low*.

Heathen, *Reality* and retirement from the stage (2000-2013)

In 2000 some sessions took place for the planned album titled *Toy*, which was supposed to be a compilation of new versions of some of Bowie's early songs with the addition of three new songs but remained unexpectedly unreleased. On August 15 of that year Alexandria Zahra "Lexie" Jones, daughter of David and Iman, was born.

In October 2001, Bowie opened the Concert for New York City, a benefit event for the victims of the September 11, 2001 terrorist attacks, with a minimalist performance of Simon & Garfunkel's song *America*, followed by the classic *"Heroes."*

Also in 2001 he played a version of *Nature Boy* for the soundtrack of the film *Moulin Rouge!*

Bowie's collaboration with Tony Visconti continued in 2002 with the production of *Heathen*, an album of previously unreleased tracks followed by the lengthy 2002

U.S. and European tour that kicked off from the Meltdown Festival in London, of which Bowie was the curator that year, inviting major artists such as Philip Glass, Television, and The Dandy Warhols.

Instead, the following year he released the album *Reality*, and the promotional tour was a great success with the public, but it was dramatically interrupted on June 25, 2004, when, after a concert at the Hurricane Festival in Scheeßel, Bowie was rushed to Hamburg for severe blockage of a coronary artery, the symptoms of which had been felt days before. Following the coronary angioplasty operation Bowie returned to New York, but the remaining eleven tour dates were canceled.

In the following years Bowie stayed away from the stage, except for a few rare appearances, however, he devoted himself to recording a few pieces for film, such as his old hit *Changes* as a duet with Butterfly Boucher for the 2004 animated film *Shrek 2* and wrote the 2005 song *(She Can) Do That*, made with Brian Transeau, for the film *Stealth - Supreme Weapon.*

He returned to perform live on September 8, 2005, with Arcade Fire for the U.S. television event *Fashion Rocks* and joined the Canadian band again a week later for the CMJ Music Marathon. A few months later he sang on a track on TV on the Radio's *Return to Cookie Mountain* album,

On February 8, 2006, he was awarded the Grammy Award for Lifetime Achievement, and after announcing in April that he would stay away from the stage for a year, he made a surprise appearance on May 29 at David Gilmour's concert at the Royal Albert Hall in London.Some of the songs from the event were recorded for the DVD *Remember That Night: Live at the Royal Albert Hall.*

His last live concert was in November 2006 with Alicia Keys for a benefit show at the Black Ball in New York City. In the same year, he participated as an actor in Christopher Nolan's film *The Prestige* as Nikola Tesla.

In 2007 he recorded a commercial with Snoop Dogg for American broadcaster XM Satellite Radio and collaborated with Lou Reed on the Danish rock group Kashmir's album *No Balance Palace.* However, his artistic commitments continued, and in the same year Bowie was chosen as artistic director of the High Line Festival in Manhattan, and he collaborated on Scarlett Johansson's album *Anywhere I Lay My Head*, which features *covers of* Tom Waits. On the 40th anniversary of the Apollo 11 moon landing, EMI released tracks from the original recording of *Space Oddity in* 2009 in a competition to which the public was invited to record a remix.

In January 2010, the double live album *A Reality Tour* was released, containing material recorded during the last tour in 2003 and 2004.

On Jan. 21, 2009, news spread on some blogs that Bowie was in Berlin recording a new album, but a denial came immediately and was also published on the artist's official website.

In March 2011, it was possible to download from the Internet the unreleased album *Toy, the* release of which had been canceled in 2001, which contains some of the songs used for *Heathen* and most of the B-sides of singles from the same record.

In 2012, Louis Vuitton hired him as a new testimonial for its new 2013 American campaign.

The return with *The Next Day* (2013-2015)

After a ten-year absence (a couple of which he spent with Visconti secretly working on new songs), on January 8, 2013, his 66th birthday, Bowie announced his new album, *The Next* Day; preceded on the same day by the single and related video for *Where Are We Now?* made by Tony Oursler, followed by *The Stars (Are Out Tonight)*, which was released on February 25. The album was released the following March 12 to great public and critical acclaim, topping the charts worldwide. On November 5, *The Next Day Extra* was released, a special version of the album also containing a DVD with video clips of *Where are we now?*, The *Stars are out Tonight*, *The Next Day* and

Valentine's Day and four previously unreleased songs in addition to the standard edition.

In the fall of 2014 Bowie released a new anthology, *Nothing Has Changed*; it was released in several formats and contains an unreleased track, *Sue (In the Season of Crime)*, also released as a single. The album achieved considerable success, especially in Europe and especially in the United Kingdom, where Bowie has always had the "hard core" of his fans. It reached ninth place in the UK charts and was awarded a gold disc after a few months for having sold over 100 000 copies.

In October 2015, John Giddins, a longtime London concert organizer, revealed that Bowie would no longer perform live and would not undertake any more tours, not even to promote *The Next Day*.

The last album *Blackstar* and death (2015-2016)

On November 19, 2015, Bowie launched his new single *Blackstar*, the first excerpt from the album of the same name, and later *Lazarus*, also accompanied by its video clip broadcast online three days before his death. Under the same title on December 12 debuted the musical of the same name written and produced for Broadway by Robert Fox, for whose theatrical premiere Bowie attended, making his last public appearance. On January

8, 2016, his 69th birthday, the studio album *Blackstar* (stylized as ★) was released.

Two days later, on the night of Jan. 10-11, the singer died suddenly, at the age of 69, in his penthouse at 285 Lafayette Street in New York City, where it is speculated he availed himself of a planned euthanasia practice due to the irremediable worsening of a liver tumor, against which he had been secretly battling for some 18 months. The news was publicized on his official Facebook profile, while in the following days Bowie's own producer Robert Fox, a friend of Bowie's, revealed that the artist had confided in him that he wanted to undertake a new experimental cancer treatment. He further recounted that only a few friends and family members were aware of his illness, but that just as many people, among those involved in recording the album, were unaware of the diagnosis until the artist's death.

According to producer Tony Visconti's statement during an interview with *RS America*, Bowie was inspired by rapper Kendrick Lamar's *To Pimp a Butterfly* album and was influenced by groups such as Death Grips and Boards of Canada. Visconti would also declare the true nature of most of the lyrics of the unreleased tracks contained in *Blackstar*, which would refer to Bowie's illness and the possibility of his imminent death, so much so that it would lead audiences to conceive of the entire project as his spiritual testament, a sort of final farewell to his audience.

On January 12, 2016, *Blackstar* debuted at the top of the U.K. Official Albums Chart, selling more than 146,000 copies and being certified gold disc in just under a day after its release. The album quickly made its mark on the world's major charts, reaching the top position in 35 countries, including Australia, Belgium, France, Germany, Ireland, the Netherlands, Sweden, Denmark, Canada, Finland, Argentina, Italy, New Zealand, and the United States, where it debuted at the No. 1 position on the Billboard 200 with 130 000 copies sold in its first week, Bowie's previous unprecedented achievement in such a short time. Bowie's catalog of all videos received over 51 million views in twenty-four hours on Vevo on January 11, surpassing the record held by Adele on the day of *Hello*'s release, while a few days later Amazon.com revealed that it had sold out every edition, both vinyl and CD format of his albums, and had never recorded such a number of sales in such a short time.

Many personalities from the music world participated in the mourning: on January 13, during one of his concerts in Los Angeles, Elton John interrupted the show's set list to pay tribute to the rock star. On Jan. 12, Madonna, on the Houston leg of her *Rebel Heart Tour,* also wanted to remember him with a cover of *Rebel Rebel*.

Mick Jagger recalled on behalf of the Rolling Stones on Twitter what Bowie was to him and the group: a "wonderful and kind man."

On the day of his death Facebook, Instagram, and Twitter quickly registered a strong flow of information and message exchanges. Millions of fans but also many music, entertainment, and political figures (including David Cameron, Brian Eno, Ariana Grande, Brian May, Bryan Adams, Bruce Springsteen, J.K. Rowling, U2, Kanye West, Paul McCartney, Martin Scorsese, and Barack Obama) expressed grief over the singer's death, leaving dedications, condolence messages to family members, photographs, and videos on the web.

On Jan. 14, some major U.S. newspapers spread the news that Bowie's remains had been cremated two days earlier in New Jersey, according to his arrangements, that is, without any suffrage rites or the presence of family and friends. Later, through a statement on Facebook, the singer's family, children and close friends thanked fans for the solidarity and affection shown and announced that they would hold a strictly private personal memorial service.

Indeed, despite numerous spontaneous initiatives around the world, there was no official public commemoration, with the exception of a large concert planned at Carnegie Hall, which had already been scheduled before his death but had now become a tribute to his memory and whose tickets, which sold out quickly, reached incredible numbers. However, the singer's family clarified that such an event was not proposed or organized by them, continuing to maintain the strictest confidentiality about the incident. Given the large expected turnout, the organizers of the tribute added the April 1 date to the planned March 31 date; this double Bowie tribute was attended by many artists including: Michael Stipe, Blondie, Cyndi Lauper, Mumford & Sons, Pixies and his friend Tony Visconti.

On January 29, 2016, some newspapers made known the terms of Bowie's holographic will, which he filed with the well-known lawyer Herbert E. Nass and signed "David Robert Jones." It stipulated the cremation of the body and the scattering of the ashes, for the latter indicating as a place the island of Bali, which Bowie visited several times, or other place of his choice closer provided Buddhist ritual was observed. The will also stipulated the division of the estate of about $100 million, half of which was earmarked for his widow Iman, also including the majority of the shares in Isolar Enterprises and the large penthouse at 285 Lafayette Street, and the remaining half, a quarter each, to his eldest son Duncan and second daughter Lexie, to whom the large property in the Catskills was also earmarked. Also benefiting from the inheritance were Corinne "Coco" Schwab, his personal assistant for more than 30 years, to whom $2 million and part of the shares of Isolar Enterprises went, and Marion Skene, the elderly nanny, to whom $1 million was paid and who died in March 2017.

Bowie's record label staff also reported that the proceeds from *Blackstar* collected throughout the month of January 2016 were donated entirely to cancer research.

An EP, titled *No Plan, was* released on January 8, 2017, the day on which Bowie would have turned 70. Except for *Lazarus*, the EP includes three songs recorded by Bowie during the sessions for the *Blackstar* album, but left off the record and later included in the soundtrack of the musical *Lazarus* in October 2016. A video clip was made for the title track.

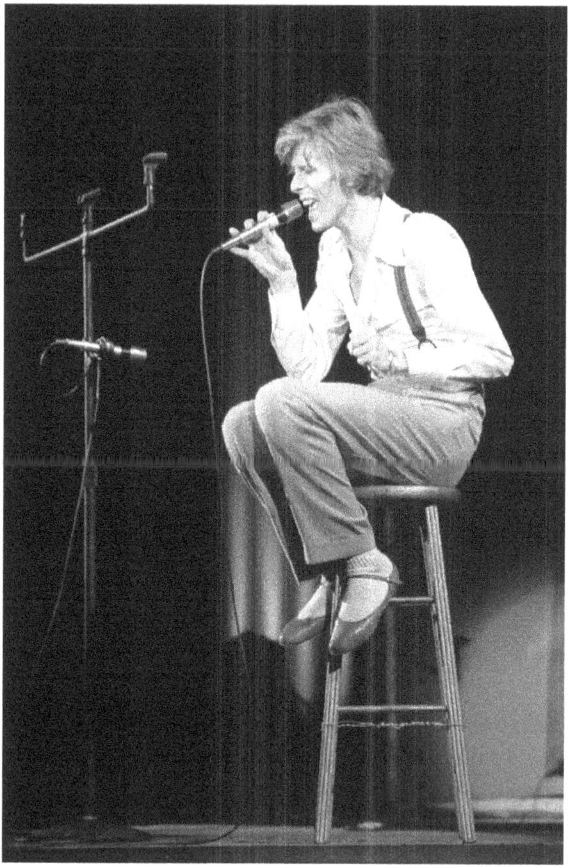

Musical style

Although he is often placed among glam rock, art rock, and new wave artists, David Bowie's style is very difficult to classify uniquely.

Initially, Bowie's musical output was based on nostalgic sounds influenced by the beat generation with acoustic folk rock songs, which would be followed by the metamorphosis of the 1970s that led Bowie to become one of the earliest and most important exponents of glam rock with albums such as *The Rise and Fall of Ziggy Stardust and the Spiders from Mars* (1972) and *Aladdin Sane* (1973).

During the 1970s, Bowie's style changed countless times, becoming more intimate and inspired several times by progressive rock, dance rock, of which he was a forerunner, and proto-punk. Confirming the eclecticism of these years are the somber *The Man Who Sold the World* (1970) and *Station to Station* (1976), the more pop *Hunky Dory* (1971), *Young Americans* (1975), which, in a sudden change of style, shifted the focus to the soul genre with the creation of white soul, and the "Berlin Trilogy" (consisting of *Low*, *"Heroes"* and *Lodger*), considered his most experimental and avant-garde phase. During the latter, Bowie was also influenced by krautrock and experimental rock, interpreting the trends, unease and turmoil typical of the time, but also anticipating the "new wave" of the years to come.

After the great pop success of the 1980s well represented by 1983's *Let's Dance*, Bowie's style returned to new experimentation, first with the formation of the group Tin Machine, started in the late 1980s, in which Bowie proposed a hard rock that has been described as "metallic." Further on, with experimental forays into electronica and industrial on the 1995 album *1.Outside*, to ranging to jungle and techno style on the 1997 album *Earthling.*

Since the 2000s, Bowie's musical style returned to a refined rock style, though without betraying the typically Brit pop sounds of his origins; however, in recent albums there is no lack of more introverted tracks with a vague new wave style. In fact, the latest album, *Blackstar* (2016), sees the artist try his hand at almost avant-garde tracks, a factor perhaps also due to the jazz and experimental background of the ensemble with which the record was made.

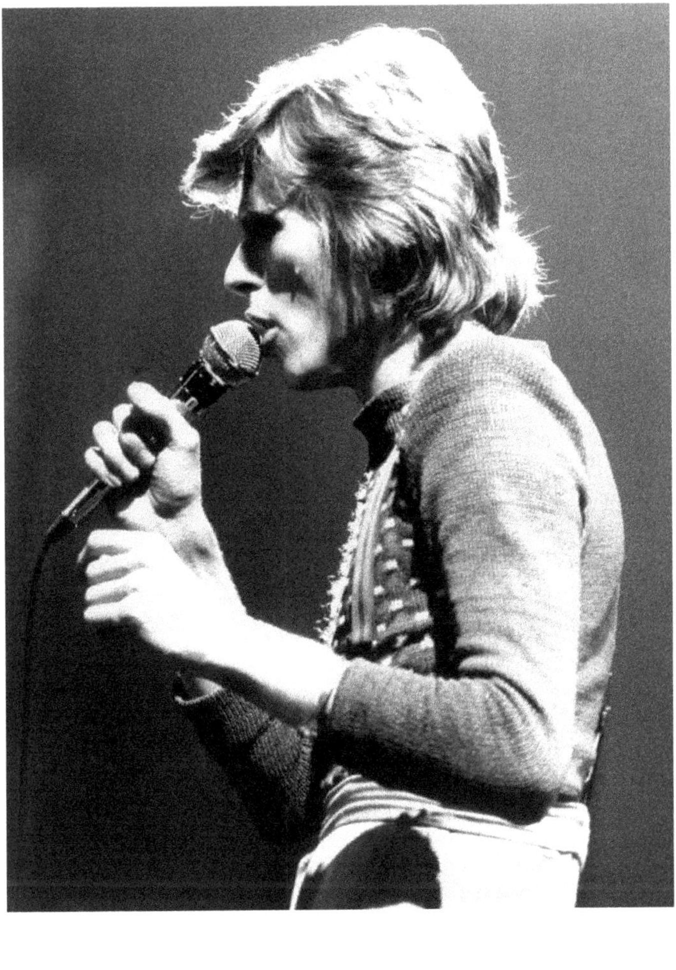

Collaborations

In addition to the aforementioned collaborations with Lou Reed, Iggy Pop, and Brian Eno, Bowie collaborated with Bing Crosby in a Christmas duet singing *Peace on Earth/Little Drummer Boy* for the 1977 television program *Merrie Olde Christmas.* However, the song was kept in the archives by RCA, Bowie's record label at the time, until in 1982, before Bowie left RCA for EMI, it was released as a single.The record reached No. 3 on the U.K. charts and became, over the years, a Christmas classic, both as a song and as a video.

Also significant was his collaboration with John Lennon on a cover of the *Beatles*' song *Across the Universe* and on *Fame*, one of Bowie's most successful songs, included on the 1975 album Young Americans.

In 1981, Bowie collaborated with Queen to record an almost unknown and unreleased version of the song *Cool Cat* and to create *Under Pressure*, in which he duetted with the British rock group and also sang at the Freddie Mercury Tribute Concert along with Annie Lennox and the Mercury-orphaned Queen themselves. The song, initially called *People on Streets*, was composed based on a "riff" by bassist John Deacon and credited to Queen and Bowie; it was later included on the 1982 album *Hot Space*.

Other collaborations of the "White Duke" included one with Rolling Stones leader Mick Jagger. Together, in 1985, in support of the Live Aid project, they made a version of Martha & the Vandellas' song *Dancing in the Street,* the video clip of which is remembered. It is also said that between the two rock stars the bond was more than professional and that the famous song *Angie*, which the Stones made in 1973, was inspired by Angela Bowie and indirectly referred to a four-way orgy between her, David, Mick and his then-wife Bianca Pérez-Mora Macias. In the same year Bowie recorded together with Tina Turner the song *Tonight*, *title track* of the 1984 album of the same name. The two would also duet together during a date on Tina Turner's 1985 Private Dancer Tour.

With NIN, Bowie opened the Outside tour in the United States where they performed both artist's songs and band songs together. The collaboration with Trent Reznor, the band's leader with whom Bowie formed a strong friendship, saw the production of several remixes, including *I'm Afraid of Americans*, in whose video Reznor appears as a co-star.

Another collaboration was with the Pet Shop Boys in 1996, for the song *Hallo Spaceboy*: building on the success of the song, which was released as a single, Bowie performed with the Pet Shop Boys on both music programs such as *Top of the Pops* and at the prestigious 1996 BRIT Awards.

After collaborating on Placebo's debut by taking them on tour as his supporters, Bowie collaborated with them on two occasions: for the single *Without you I'm nothing*, taken from the album of the same name, they made a two-voice version, while in February 1999 they performed together at the Brit Awards for a cover of *20th Century Boy*, which Placebo by the way also played in the film *Velvet Goldmine*, as members of the fictional band Malcolm & The Flaming Creatures. The close bond between the band and Bowie was evidenced by several episodes: the tribute paid to him with an acoustic version of *Five Years* performed in 2004 during a French television program and the touching farewell letter written by Brian Molko shortly after Bowie's death and published on the band's official website.

Personal life

In 1970 he married Mary Angela Barnett with whom he had a son, Duncan Zowie Haywood Jones, in 1971; the two divorced in 1980. In 1992 he married Somali model Iman Mohamed Abdulmajid at St. James Church in Florence. By her in 2000 he had a daughter, Alexandria "Lexie" Zahra.

The debate on sexuality

In late 1964, when he was part of the Manish Boys, the group auditioned the BBC for a series of concerts at the Star Club in Hamburg. The singer secured the gig by swearing to the German organizer that he was gay. Later, despite the fact that his ostentatious ambiguous and transgressive attitudes led to speculation that he was homosexual, 16-year-old Bowie met 14-year-old Dana Gillespie, who became his girlfriend and whom he continued to date into the 1970s. In January 1972, an interview was published in *Melody Maker in which he* admitted to being gay; this created some uproar and promotional intent was speculated in preparation for the release of the new album *The Rise and Fall of Ziggy Stardust and the Spiders from Mars*. Nevertheless, the British gay movement elected David as its symbol. After all, taboos always exerted a strong attraction on Bowie, and his nonconformity pushed him into the homosexual subculture. Despite this, David's comments on the subject made in later years were anything but clarifying: " [...] *it's true, I'm bisexual,*" he told *Playboy* magazine in September 1976, except to answer another interviewer's question a short time later by stating the opposite: " [...] *it was just a lie, they stuck that image on me and I adjusted to it pretty well for a few years.*" During the 1978 tour of New Zealand he again declared that he was bisexual, instead in 1983, when Bowie was becoming an international superstar, he retracted his earlier statements, telling *Time* magazine that it had been "*a big misunderstanding,*" and in *Rolling Stone* he called it "*the biggest mistake I ever made.*" In 1987, pressed on the subject by *Smash Hits*, he amusedly pointed out the whole thing, allowing the magazine to publish, "*You shouldn't believe everything you read.*" In 1993, also in *Rolling Stone* magazine, he debunked the rumor regarding his bisexuality: " [...] I *never felt like a real bisexual but I was magnetized by the underground gay scene. It was like another reality that I wanted to buy a share of. This phase lasted only until 1974 and died more or less with Ziggy. Really, I had only made the bisexual status my own, the irony being that I was not gay.*." Eventually, however, even the latter version was changed again in 2002, justifying the earlier retractions: when *Blender* asked him if he still thought the public statement was his biggest mistake, after a long pause he replied, "*I don't think it was a problem in Europe, but it was much harder in America. I had no problem with people knowing I was bisexual, but I had no inclination to hold banners or represent a group of people.*"

Discography

David Bowie's discography consists of 25 studio albums as a solo artist and two with the Tin Machine group of which he was a member. Bowie himself before his death, in a letter to Brian Eno, referred to his last work as his 25th album. It also includes four soundtracks, five EPs, 15 live albums, 50 compilations and 113 singles. One estimate put his output at about 720 songs, with a total of 147 million albums sold worldwide.

Studio albums

- 1967 - *David Bowie*
- 1969 - *Space Oddity*
- 1970 - *The Man Who Sold the World*
- 1971 - *Hunky Dory*
- 1972 - *The Rise and Fall of Ziggy Stardust and the Spiders from Mars.*
- 1973 - *Aladdin Sane*
- 1973 - *Pin Ups*
- 1974 - *Diamond Dogs*
- 1975 - *Young Americans*
- 1976 - *Station to Station*
- 1977 - *Low*
- 1977 - *"Heroes"*
- 1979 - *Lodger*

- 1980 - *Scary Monsters (and Super Creeps)*
- 1983 - *Let's Dance*
- 1984 - *Tonight*
- 1987 - *Never Let Me Down*
- 1993 - *Black Tie White Noise*
- 1995 - *1.Outside*
- 1997 - *Earthling*
- 1999 - *'hours...'*
- 2002 - *Heathen*
- 2003 - *Reality*
- 2013 - *The Next Day*
- 2016 - *Blackstar*
- 2021 - *Toy* (posthumous)

With the Tin Machine
- 1989 - *Tin Machine*
- 1991 - *Tin Machine II*

Live Albums
- 1974 - *David Live*
- 1978 - *Internship*
- 1983 - *Ziggy Stardust - The Motion Picture.*
- 1992 - *Tin Machine Live: Oy Vey, Baby* (with Tin Machine)
- 1999 - *LiveAndWell.com.*
- 2008 - *Live Santa Monica '72*
- 2009 - *VH1 Storytellers*
- 2010 - *A Reality Tour*
- 2017 - *Live Nassau Coliseum '76*

- 2017 - *Cracked Actor (Live Los Angeles '74)*
- 2018 - *Welcome to the Blackout (Live London '78)*
- 2018 - *Glastonbury 2000*
- 2019 - *Serious Moonlight (Live '83)*
- 2019 - *Glass Spider (Live Montréal '87)*
- 2019 - *Ouvre le Chien (Live Dallas 95)*
- 2020 - *Something in the Air (Live Paris 99)*
- 2020 - *I'm Only Dancing (The Soul Tour 74)*
- 2020 - *No Trendy Réchauffé (Live Birmingham 95)*

Soundtracks
- 1980 - *Christiane F. - We, the boys from the Berlin Zoo*
- 1986 - *Labyrinth*
- 1986 - *Absolute Beginners*
- 1993 - *The Buddha of Suburbia*
- 2016 - *Lazarus*

Videography

Forever recognized as one of the pioneers of the music video, as early as 1969 Bowie had enough promos under his belt to put together a feature film, even before he had scored his first chart-topping hit with a single. His first video clip was that of the song *Space Oddity*, released in 1972 and directed by Mick Rock.

Bowie's videography includes 71 promotional video clips to add to four other videos by other artists in which he participated, 15 album or compilation videos released on VHS, DVD, and 18 guest appearances in videos by other artists.

More recent creations such as *The Hearts Filthy Lesson*, *Little Wonder*, and *Survive* have confirmed that Bowie continues to explore the boundaries of the music video. In the new millennium, collaborations with directors such as Floria Sigismondi and Johan Renck and Hollywood actors such as Gary Oldman and Tilda Swinton have brought Bowie's video clips closer to true cinematic shorts.

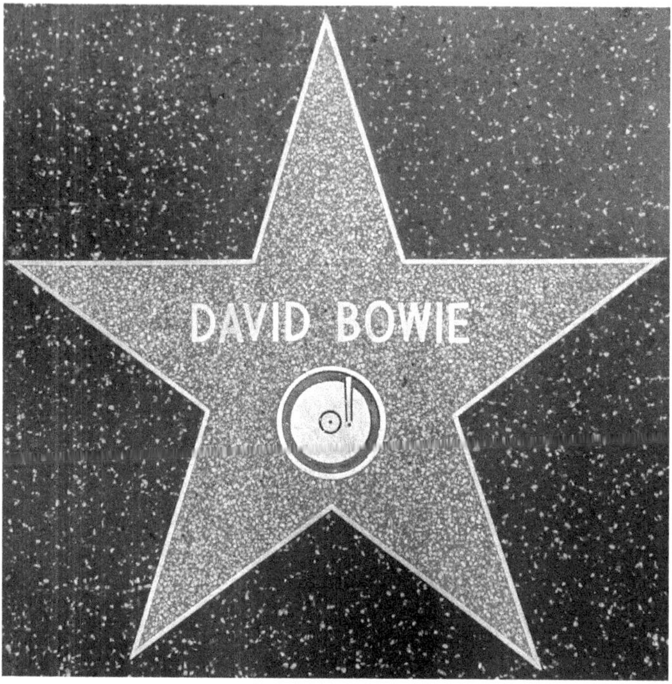
DAVID BOWIE

Other books by United Library

https://campsite.bio/unitedlibrary

Milton Keynes UK
Ingram Content Group UK Ltd.
UKHW020814080324
439029UK00015B/785